BRENDAN BEHAN

The Scarperer

HUTCHINSON OF LONDON

HUTCHINSON & CO (*Publishers*) LTD
178–202 Great Portland Street, London W1

London Melbourne Sydney
Auckland Bombay Toronto
Johannesburg New York

★

First published 1966

*This book has been set in Garamond, printed in Great Britain
on Antique Wove paper by Anchor Press, and
bound by Wm. Brendon, both of Tiptree, Essex*

Foreword by Rae Jeffs

On October 19th, 1953, the *Irish Times* newspaper announced the publication of the first instalment of a serial about Dublin's underworld, *The Scarperer* by Emmet Street. It ran for thirty days and nothing further was heard of the author.

Nothing further indeed might ever have been heard of the author, had it not been for a chance remark I made to Brendan in 1962.

I was being slightly disparaging about a well-known crime writer, when Brendan told me that at one time he would have agreed with me. Since then, however, he had tried his hand at writing a crime story and had not found it quite so easy.

When I asked to see it, he astounded me by telling me that it had already been published. Where? As a serial in the *Irish Times*. He couldn't remember exactly when and he certainly did not have a copy of it (Brendan never kept a copy of anything he wrote).

He did remember, however, that 'I wrote it under the phoney name of Emmet Street, which was the name of the street opposite the one I was reared in, in North Dublin. And I wrote it under another name for the following reason:

'I had started writing for Irish Republican and Irish Left Wing newspapers and, up to this, the Dublin intelligentsia were very friendly disposed towards me, because I had published very little. And for a garrulous man, one of the very few things I talk about is my own writing.

'By 1953, I was quite well-known as a poet and a writer, and unfortunately the Dublin intelligentsia had seen pieces of pornography that I'd written for French magazines when I was in France—in English, of course. This didn't exactly endear me to them, so being short of the readies, I decided to write under a phoney name.'

Brendan explained that he sent the first draft of the story to the *Irish Times,* who immediately accepted it but would not give him an advance. With what little money he had—which was practically nothing—he went to the Aran Islands to write the story in peace and without fear of interruption. Within a few days his money was gone. He wired the *Irish Times* to this effect to enable him to finish it.

A few hours later, he collected ninety pounds from the post office. The *Irish Times* had not failed him and he was never to forget it.

Back in Dublin for the publication, Brendan went round the various pubs in Grafton Street, literally the fashionable centre of Dublin, to hear what the 'intelligentsia' thought of this new Irish writer. Apparently they liked him.

Tracing the serial proved more of an obstacle than I had thought, but eventually with the help of Jack White, the Literary Editor of the *Irish Times* at the time and now with *Radio Eireann,* I found it.

It is part of the tragedy that Brendan did not live to see the publication of *The Scarperer* for the first time under its rightful author's name. He knew, of course, that it was to appear. It is a story of which he was particularly fond and one which he thoroughly enjoyed writing, with the added kick of knowing it was a hoax. Although obviously of a lighter vein, much of the talent that was shortly to produce

The Quare Fellow, The Hostage and *Borstal Boy* can be clearly seen in this, his only novel. It is a neat plot, cleverly constructed, and reveals one further piece of evidence of his extraordinary versatility.

²scarp \\'skärp, 'skȧp\ *n* -s [It. *scarpa*, prob. of Gmc orgin; akin to OE *scearp* sharp—more at SHARP]
1: a nearly vertical sometimes walled side of a ditch below the parapet of a fortification–called also *escarp;* compare COUNTERSCARP **2a:** a line of cliffs produced by faulting or erosion—see FAULT-LINE SCARP **b:** a low steep slope along a beach caused by wave erosion.

³scarp \\'"\ *vt* -ED -ING -S: to cut so as to form a scarp: cut down vertically or to a steep slope ⟨ ～ the face of a ditch ⟩ ⟨ ～ a coast into rugged cliffs ⟩.

scarp·er –'skȧpə(r\ *vi* -ED -ING -S [perh. fr. It. *scappare* to flee, escape, fr. (assumed) VL *excappare*—more at ESCAPE] *Brit.:* to run away: make off.

I

A<small>T THE</small> Morning Star it was rumoured that Dunlavin had won it. But at the Mendicity that morning, the queue waiting for breakfast were told by a fellow from Navan that Tralee Trembles owned the ticket.

Nancy Hand, on the women's side of the lane, said from her queue that it was all equal which of them had won it. Both of them were Culchiemocks, and anything that was going in the city they were bound to get it. Them or the Northerns.

From round her in the women's queue there was some bad language used about Dublin so-and-sos, while Nancy looked about her in defiance. From the men's queue, a Kerry accent rose in plaintive protest, and Craigavad told them not to give no heed till that dirty oul'——

Nancy didn't even wait for it:

'Dirty oul' what? Dirty oul' what, you rotten Northerner?' and so forth, till she turned her attention to the Kerryman, and called his attention to the state of his shoes.

'Yous scruffy lot of bogmen. Bogmen and Orangemen, them's the only ones there's a bit of respect for in this town. And the people here too soft for yous. Don't I remember meself Daggers Doyle coming home from Chicago after the boxing, and people out along Gardiner Street and a banner the width of Waterford Street, the same one they used in the Congress, with Saint Patrick in green whiskers playing a harp on one side and "Play up, Shels" on the other, to welcome Daggers Doyle back from America. And sure that fellow's mother is from Kilcock, and our own decent Irishmen walking the streets and not a word about them.'

Some of the men shouted across at her, and a voice came from behind in the women's queue.

'Let me go, and I'll be dug out of her.'

'Leave her go, then,' said Nancy, 'and you needn't take your coat off, Kilbeggan Kate, for I'll beat it off you.'

Someone shouted the man was coming to let them in and there was a moment's peace, till the door opened and they went in to breakfast.

'I suppose,' said Craigavad to the Mendicity man when he brought round the porridge, 'that Tralee Trembles nor Dunlavin wouldn't be likely to come round here?'

'They would not then,' said the Mendicity man, 'and if they did itself, they wouldn't get past that door. I sent Dunlavin for a can of porridge one day and caught him stirring it, so as I wouldn't miss the milk he was after pouring off the top and drinking; and I wouldn't have minded so much but he was using that old walking-stick of his to stir it with. And as for Tralee Trembles, he never came here only to sell his breakfast for the price of a glass of a chat.'

'Who won the Sweep?' asked the Mendicity.

'Well some says it was Dunlavin and more that it was Tralee Trembles' ticket, but we don't know for sure,' said Craigavad. 'Not till we go up to the Hot-Wall and find out.'

'The Hot-Wall?'

'It's where the boys do go. The side-wall of a bakery off of Thomas Street. It's where the ovens are behind it and it does be lovely and hot. Better nor the Gresham. But you'd want your place booked in the real winter. This weather it's easy enough to get a stand.'

'Thanks,' said the Mendicity man, 'I'll let you know when I'm wanting one.'

'And it does be handy for the boys out of the Spike to dodge out for the result of the Sweep.'

'The Sweep Dunlavin won, or Tralee Trembles?'

'Yes. All the shams, they put in threepence of a night with Pig's Eye O'Donnell, and he gets a mot, someone we know like, to draw a paper out of a hat. Dunlavin or Tralee Trembles won it last night, but the draw was in the Shaky Man's and they were in some other chat-shop and they mightn't even know yet.'

A man banged his spoon on the table.

'Hey, are you going to spend your youth giving us the bit of skilly, or do you want your mug stuck in it?'

'*Excuse me,*' said the Mendicity man, 'one of me clients seems to want service.'

Dunlavin it was. Tralee Trembles was only minding the ticket for him, because Dunlavin was lobby-watching this weather. He was barred in most of the lodging houses, and the ones he was let into were all full, so he slept on the landings of tenement houses and spent the price of his flop, when he had it, on chat. He had lately lost a pair of boots, given him at the mission, and Tralee Trembles took the ticket on account of him having a flop nearly always.

Nobody minded Trembles. He was quiet enough, only when he was in jig street he might see the devil in the middle of the night, but a kick in the ribs would settle that.

The pay-out was in the Shaky Man's, and not a one missing for whatever drop might be stirring. Pig's Eye paid out like a man. Two pounds and ten shillings, and collected threepence a skull off the people for the next Sweep. Even the Shaky Man took a couple of tickets for, as Pig's Eye said, if you never put it down you never picked it up, and you must speculate to accumulate.

Dunlavin's eyes were far out of his head, looking at the money. And Tralee Trembles beside him.

'Eh, Dunlavin, I minded the ticket for you. Didn't I mind it well, and give it good care?'

Dunlavin was looking up at Pig's Eye.

'God bless you, Mister O'Donnell. Or Pig's Eye, if I can call you be your Christian name. May the giving hand never falter.'

'Ah, don't mind that, Dunlavin. I'm only giving you what's your own. Didn't you take your chance like a man?'

'He did that,' said Nancy Hand, looking round in defiance, 'deny it who will.'

'And, Dunlavin, didn't I mind the ticket?'

'You did, Tralee Trembles, you did. And I'm not forgetting. You'll get a drink and so will everybody.'

A cheer went up.

'More power, Dunlavin, the height of luck to you. I wouldn't doubt you. Glasses of chat.'

'Glasses of chat,' said Dunlavin, 'what use is that? No, but bottles of it.'

'Fair enough, Mr. Dunlavin,' said the Shaky Man, holding up a bottle for inspection.

'The Royal Tawny Port, as supplied to Her Majesty, the Queen Mother of Portugal, at two and four the bottle—a dozen to begin with will be twenty-eight shillings.'

'That's all right; I'll fix that.'

A well-dressed man of about thirty-six stepped forward. No one saw him come in, though for the matter of that, no one was watching the door.

Pig's Eye seemed to know him. And fear him, and be surprised to see him. He spoke in a whisper.

'It's Eddie—Eddie Collins! But I th-thought you were the other side—in the shovel—in Parkhurst—on the island—I——'

The stranger's eyes narrowed and very intently he looked into Pig's Eye's eyes.

'Shut your mouth. You've a lot too much rabbit. Always had.'

'Right, sir,' said the Shaky Man, with the bottle and glasses.

The stranger took out his wallet.

'And yourself, sir?'

'I think I'll try a bottle of lemonade.'

'A bottle of——?'

'Lemonade.'

'Certainly, sir,' said the Shaky Man, looking to see who he would send to the chip-shop on the corner for it.

2

THE wine was poured, and the glasses set up.
'More power, Dunlavin.'

'More power the strange man that bought the drink. Who is he, anyway?' asked the Goofy One.

'Never you mind,' says Pig's Eye, 'or I'll let you know to be asking questions. He might hear you.'

' 'Deed he won't,' said the Goofy One, 'he's over at the counter waiting on his lemonade.'

'Right ould buff he must be,' said Nancy Hand. 'What you wouldn't give to a child.'

'Never you mind him,' said Pig's Eye. 'Just shut up your mouth.'

'Bedad and he has the heart crossways in you, anyway, Pig's Eye, if he drinks lemonade itself, whoever he is. You're the colour of a corpse that's not in its health.'

'I'll leave you a corpse,' said Pig's Eye, between his teeth, 'if you don't mind yourself.' He brought his foot and all his weight to bear on her toes.

'Oh,' cried Nancy Hand, with a look of agony, 'stand on your own———'

Pig's Eye looked at her again, and she said no more.

The stranger's lemonade was slipped over the counter and the Shaky Man poured it.

'Sorry for the delay, sir. Stuff on the shelves has run out and I had to send to the cellar for some more.'

'That's all right. Big run on lemonade this weather.'

14

'Do you often come round here, sir?'

'Do you call this boozer the *Old Curiosity Shop*?'

'Eh, no, sir, certainly not, sir. It's only——'

'Only what?'

'It's only like that, sir, if you were, I could always have lemonade or that ready, sir. A man likes to please his customers, if you know what I mean.'

'Oh, I see. Ah, I spend most of my time down the country and if I come again, I'll know where to call. I like it here. It's nice and cosy.'

In the corner Nancy Hand was preparing to do battle with a woman from the North Side.

'I don't know whether you're worth a month, but I'll get that much value out of it; they'll think you're after leaving the abattoir.'

'It's homely like, all right,' said the Shaky Man, reaching under the counter for the bung mallet.

Nancy's humour had changed for the moment. She was singing:

> 'Hand me down me petticoat,
> Hand me down me shawl,
> Hand me down me petticoat,
> For I'm off to the Linen Hall.'

Some arrangement had been come to with the North Side lady and her friends, for when Nancy finished her song, she had a noble call, which she used to demand a song about Summerhill. Meanwhile the Goofy One kept up a chant of her own, composed of two lines on the same monotone:

> 'Who was the cruel villain
>   did the simple girl betray?
> A German U-boat it came up
>   from underneath the Bay . . .'

15

'Come along, now,' shouted Nancy Hand, 'a bit of order for Mrs. Genockey, famous along the Quay, on the left-hand side as you go down, for her talent, will oblige the company.'

Mrs. Genockey gazed modestly on the floor, cleared her throat, patted the back of her head, and rolled her eyes upwards and on to the ceiling.

'Give us the one you got the six months for,' said someone, jovially encouraging from the crowd.

Her friend turned indignantly.

'Shut your ignorant mouth, yous perishing scruff. Mrs. Genockey took a prize at the Fish Coyle.'

'Only had to leave it back, when the lady searcher came round.'

Mrs. Genockey's friend turned again, but set her lips, for her friend's lips had opened and in a good round voice she was making sounds in a foreign language.

'Ah,' said Nancy Hand, rolling her head in a cultured fashion, 'the yapera. Eyetalian. I'd know it a mile away.'

Mrs. Genockey carried herself off, eyes shut, on the wings of song.

'If you want to know,' said her friend in a low, respectful voice, 'it's not the yapera, nayther is it Eyetalian.'

'What is it?'

'It's the Lord's Prayer,' she nodded impressively, 'in Welsh.'

At the counter, the stranger was arguing with Dunlavin, who wanted to buy the drinks he had promised out of his winnings.

'That's all right,' said the stranger. 'They have enough to be going on with. Just now, you and I and Mr. ——'

'They call him Tralee Trembles, sir,' said Dunlavin.

'That's right,' said Tralee, holding out his shaking hand.

'And you'll have a drink with me,' said the stranger, 'a glass of whiskey.'

16

Tralee's eyes of bleary blue widened, and it seemed for a minute that he was going to cry.

'Can I, sir?'

'You can, to be sure, and several more besides.'

And he did too, till closing time.

Outside the last of the stragglers had disappeared up the road carrying bottles and roaring or singing. Tralee was helpless against the door of the pub, and the Shaky Man inside had finished counting his money and was gone up to bed. Dunlavin was torn between loyalty to his friend and a wish to catch up with the people with the bottles before they reached the Catacombs and locked him out of the party. The stranger spoke:

'Go ahead you, Mr. Dunlavin. I'll look after this man.'

'God bless you,' said Dunlavin. 'I'm leaving him in good hands. I'll leave him with that bottle of chat. He'll need it in the morning when he's seeing the divil. Goodnight, sir.' He ran up the street calling to his friends to wait for him.

'Tralee,' whispered the stranger, 'do you often see the devil?'

'I do,' said Tralee, clutching the bottle closer to him, 'often, but don't talk about him. They say he's sure to appear.'

'*And he has,*' said the stranger quietly. '*Look in the window.*'

Tralee roused himself, turned to look into a whiskey mirror advertisement in the window. In semi-darkness, he saw his own face, wild and fearful, and a darker reflection behind peering over his shoulder. He screamed in terror, raised the bottle and smashed the glass and fell down, clutching at the path.

At the corner of the street, the stranger met a Guard.

'Sorry to trouble you, Officer, but a man up there has

17

just broken the window of the public house on the left. No need for me to go with you, I suppose?'

The Guard shook his head wearily.

'No, sir. Too well I know the place. Good-night, sir, and thanks.'

'Good-night, Guard,' said the stranger, and walked briskly towards the quays.

3

WHEN the Guard reached him, Tralee Trembles was hugging the pavement, flat out among the broken glass of the Shaky Man's shattered window. Shaky had put out his head, seen it was only the window, and gone to bed. The Guards could fix it up. It wasn't good to be charging people, and anyway, the rates would cover it.

A crowd gathered, and one of them made a half-hearted effort to waken Tralee Trembles and tell him the Guard was on his way up the street. But it wasn't much good, for Tralee was too far gone, snorting, clenching his teeth, and jumping in convulsions every few seconds.

'Something he ate,' said a young man to the Guard when he arrived.

'You just mind your business,' said the Guard in a heavy Munster accent.

'And oo mind oors,' shouted the young man, laughing as he ran off.

The crowd continued to discuss the matter.

'Someone should a told that ould fellow An Tóstal is over.'

'Come on,' said the Guard. 'Move off out of that. There's nothing to see here. Come on, get a move on with you.'

The crowd backed away a bit, but only to the darker side of the road.

'Eh, would oo work for a farmer?' someone shouted in

a mock Cork accent. 'If oo want to stand there, oo'll have to move on.'

'*Nick, Nick, the squad car.*'

The wireless patrol car was coming up from the bridge and they scattered before it reached them.

'Here, give us a hand with this fellow,' said the Guard, and Tralee Trembles was carried unconscious into the car.

'Bridewell, I suppose?' asked the driver, turning from his seat in front.

'No,' said the Guard, 'the Shelbourne Hotel.'

They drove down the street and over the bridge.

'Well,' said the station sergeant, 'is that the best you could manage? Tralee Trembles. Well, every little helps.'

To the jailer: 'Stick him in one of the cells looking out towards the flats. Away at the end. We mustn't have him disturbing the other guests when he wakes up and starts roaring at the divil.'

'What's his right name?' asked the Guard, making out a sheet. 'I can hardly put Tralee Trembles on it.'

'Oh, we have it here,' said the sergeant. 'James Guiney, native of Kerry; no business and no fixed abode. The charge is simply "drunk," I suppose?'

'No; malicious damage too. He broke a window.'

'Oh, did he? Must be getting his health. Starting to take food with his meals. Right, Number One Court in the morning.'

Tralee Trembles woke up and looked up at the barred window. He was there again. In a concrete box, with a brown painted door, solid timber with metal sheets, and a little hole for the jailer to look in at him on his rounds. A box with a wooden cover that could be let down if they wanted to pass him in a drink of water.

'Water, Jailer, a sup of water!'

Someone else took up the cry:

'Give us a drink of water!'

And the pleading stage was reached:

'Ah, Guard, please give us a drink of water, Guard, please. . . .'

Water, Tralee thought. His tongue was hard and prickly, like a hedgehog's back. *Water!* To soak in it and soften the prickles in a mug of nice cold water. . . .

He lay back on his mattress, and putting the end of his blanket on the wooden pillow to soften it for his head, looked up at the ceiling and thought of it. The ceiling was cocoa-stained. Somebody had thrown his cocoa at it. But even cocoa would be wet, wet. . . . And if the Guards were worse, now, they could make you swallow a mug of sand, or a pint of sawdust. . . .

'Water, please, a drink of water.' He was at the door and kicking and tearing at it.

The others took it up.

'Water, please, like a decent man. You dirty half-animal, give us a drink of water, water, water!'

'Shut up,' came a roar and a swinging of keys up the stairs, 'or I know what I'll give you.'

The jailer was taking up another one. They could hear him singing when his cell door was opened:

> 'They shot them in pairs
> coming down the stairs,
> At the Valley of Knockanure.'

'Get in there and shut up, or I'll put you down the stairs and up them too.' He banged the door, and his footsteps echoed in the passage and keys jangled till the noise faded and there was silence but for the chimes of Christchurch, lonely in the night, from the top of the hill.

In the morning they were brought together and left in a big cell till the court opened. There were two well-dressed screwsmen caught on a warehouse roof, down the North Wall. They talked amongst themselves in low tones, and gave Tralee Trembles a cigarette, and then resumed their own conversation. They seemed mostly concerned about the immediate problem of bail. Though, having previous form, they stood to get three to five years. That was a long way off, and they had dates that night for the 4 P's.

There was a man in for not maintaining his wife, and a boy of fourteen who had broken gas-meters. A young man from a respectable suburb, who had taken a loan of some-one's car to get home from a dance, wept bitterly. The others tried to console him, telling him it was a first offence, and, as he said he was college-educated, he was bound to get off with a fine, or maybe the Probation Act—certainly not the shovel.

'The—the what?' he asked fearfully.

'The shovel and pick, the nick. The 'Joy.¹ Jail.'

'Oh, but it's not that. It's the disgrace of being up in court.'

After that they felt they could do no more for him.

Tralee Trembles was up in the dock but a few minutes. The judge asked him why he broke the window and Tralee said he had seen the devil in it.

'Funny district for him to be. Not much for him there. I'd have thought Foxrock was nearer the mark.'

The clerk, who up to this had given His Worship the rapt attention of a Sunday-school pupil, and the Guards, who stood stern and strong, as if physical assault was threatening His Worship and they were there to die in his defence, all laughed, quiet behind their hands, as if they couldn't help it.

The records' man, who had a pleasant face and looked

1. Mountjoy Prison

kindly and intelligent, leaned over and whispered something to the justice.

'I see, I see,' said the justice, and then to Tralee: 'Well now, James Guiney, I think we'll have the doctor to have a look at you. Right, remanded seven days for medical examination.'

As Tralee Trembles left the dock, the stranger, known to Pig's Eye O'Donnell as Eddie Collins, left his place in the gallery behind, and went down the street, into the telephone kiosk on Arran Quay and dialled a number.

'That you, Scarperer? Yes. OK. Medical remand for seven days. Yes, of course he'll go in the hospital. I was afraid too. Thought they might send him to the 'Gorman.[1] Thanks, always glad to do a bit. Yes, meet you for lunch and a few drinks. Somewhere well out of town. I'll use a taxi. Leave my own car where it is.'

1. Grangegorman, a mental hospital

4

TRALEE TREMBLES sat in a cell, on the side of the bed, a cigarette about three-fifths from his nose, staring into it, as if mesmerised. Now and again he shook, and the ash fell to the floor. He sat for a couple of hours till a policeman came to the door and shouted in:

'Your carriage awaits, Tralee. Put out your butt, and we'll be off to the old house and just in time for lunch.'

Tralee smiled, for civility's sake, and followed the Guard up to the charge-room to sign for his property; a piece of a comb, a shoe-lace, a copy of a pamphlet entitled, 'Lay sanctity or a shield against worldly temptations for the ordinary plain business man,' and three pennies and a halfpenny in coppers. The Guard put them all in an envelope stamped 'Eire' over a harp, and added it to a collection in his satchel.

'Brilliant man,' murmured the Guard to the others behind the desk. 'Schoolmaster once. Only for this,' making the motion of one lowering a glass. 'Father was one of the biggest pig-blockers in Castle Island, only for the ould ——,' and he repeated the action.

'Many a good man's case,' said the sergeant.

'His son was a poet too, in his day, weren't you, Tralee?'

'I was that,' said Tralee Trembles with a sigh. 'Won a competition in *Old Moore's Almanac,* and had poetry printed in *Ireland's Own*—twice.'

24

'Before we go out to the ould yoke,' said the Guard, with indulgent pride in his prodigy, 'say one of your poems to the men.'

'I haven't anything about me at the moment,' said Tralee Trembles, 'but I'll say one I translated from the Latin.'

'Go ahead, so,' says the sergeant.

'You're the man that'll appreciate it,' said the Guard.

Tralee put his head back and spoke evenly:

'There is sadness in my sadness when I'm sad.
There is a gladness in my gladness when I'm glad.
There is a madness in my madness when I'm mad.
But the sadness in my sadness,
And the gladness in my gladness . . .'

'And the madness in your madness,' murmured the sergeant respectfully.

'. . . Are nothing to my badness when I'm bad.'

'There's for you now,' said the Guard, 'but come on, Tralee, we have to be off.'

''Morrow, men,' said the sergeant, sighing, as they walked out into the yard. 'A terrible pity, but it seems to be the way with all these geniuses. Too much in here'—he tapped the side of his head significantly—'and it has to come out somewhere.'

'Well, it's either that or turning agin religion,' said the duty-man.

''Tis true for you,' said the sergeant, more cheerfully, 'and sure God knows that'd be worse.'

'Get in there, Tralee, and make yourself comfortable.'

There was a boy sitting near the door, and he shouted at him to move up out of that. There was plenty of room, but the boy moved an inch or two and Tralee sat in. One of

25

the other prisoners handed him a lighted cigarette and he put it in his mouth, gazing on the end of it. The Guard slammed the door dividing the driver's compartment from the prisoners, and they moved off.

The women's compartment was separated from the men's by a wooden partition running the length of the waggon.

There were slits at the top for ventilation, and the boy and one of the other prisoners stood up to look out, and commented wistfully on the district passed through.

'Green Street ball alley,' said the boy.

'That's where they have the fullies,' said the prisoner that gave Tralee the cigarette.

'What's them?' said the boy.

'You'll be finding out soon enough if you don't keep your hands easy. It's the C.C.C.—the Central Criminal Court.'

'Oh,' said the boy.

'That's where they tried Robert Emmet,' said the other prisoner, a quiet man, in over wife maintenance.

'How did he get on?' asked the boy, politely. And excitedly, 'Oh, look out, we're going past the Plaza now, the picture-house. Smashing follyer-upper. I go to it every Sunday. Never miss it.'

'Well, you're going to miss it next Sunday.'

'I suppose I am,' said the boy quietly, his mouth working a little.

The maintenance man looked at the other prisoner sternly.

'Ah, sure it's only a bottle of smoke, son. You'll be out and about before you know where you are. Where are we now, be the same token?'

'I think,' said the boy, importantly—'wait now, we're slowing up. We're at—yes, I'm right, we're at Dorset Street traffic lights.'

'Won't be long now.'

26

'No, just up Blessington Street, round Berkeley Road, down the North Circular, and we're home and dried.'

One of the women was shouting from the other side:

'Oh, I love the cops and the cops love me,
And the blessing of God on the D.M.G.'

And some other remarks in the chorus, which caused the Guard in the front to bang back indignantly on the timber for her to shut up.

She turned her attention to the people in the street, with screeches and shouts.

'Yous'll never beat the Irish out of Ireland. Are you in there, Tralee?' And she explained to her friends, 'Poor old Tralee, no harm in him, he's a wine victim, y'know.'

'Certainly we do,' came the reply, 'and what's more, we understand. He's what is called a cider-baron, am I right, Concepta?'

A drowsy muttering answered, 'Let me off. I'm past me stop.'

'It's the Goofy One,' said Concepta. 'She's awake.'

'So she is,' said the other one, 'she's coming to. Eh, give us a bar of an old song before we get into the old house.'

The Goofy One cleared her throat, and sang:

'How much is the doggy in the window?
And remember our glorious dead.'

'More power the Goofy One,' said the others. 'I wouldn't doubt you.'

The van slowed up.

'We're going round.'

In the men's compartment, the boy said from the ventilation slit, 'We're there.'

'No, we're not yet,' said the maintenance man. 'This is the Female.'

'That's right,' shouted Concepta through the partition. 'Ladies first.'

The van stopped and the women's side of the door was opened.

Concepta shouted a farewell. 'Up the blue room.'

The maintenance man answered her. 'Don't take any bad money.'

The door was banged and they drove down and round, and up the avenue to the main gate.

There were shouts from the driver to the warders at the gate, the gate opened and the van moved forward.

The boy turned his head from the ventilation slit, and said very quietly to himself, 'We're going in.'

5

THE main gate opened and the warder shouted in to the man on the inner gate. The van drove slowly in and stopped in the yard, opposite the steps leading to the prison.

The Guard opened the door and shouted: 'Put out them cigarettes, where do you think you are? And hurry up, get out.'

They filed out and stood in a line beside the van.

A warder stood with the Guard, speaking to him.

The boy looked around him. There were prisoners weeding round a grass verge. They wore heavy frieze suits, dark grey, with a broad stripe, and caps of the same colour, with a large button on top. Other prisoners passed by wheeling a cart full of laundry. They wore no jackets, but cotton shirts, and a heavy brown piece of cloth round the neck to represent a tie.

The boy whispered to the maintenance man, and the warder shouted without turning his head: 'Cut out the talking, where d'you think you are?'

A short, powerfully built man with a heavy shock of grey hair came down the steps, followed by a man dressed in a warder's uniform, with a silver band round his cap. The Guard nudged the warder, who stiffened to attention, raised his hand to the peak of his cap in salute, and shouted: 'Four receptions, all correct, sir.'

The grey-haired man nodded, and went on up the path.

'Right. All you, follow me,' said the warder.

'Follow the man, when he tells yous,' said the Guard, though they had already started. He walked behind them. Down a few steps to the left of the prison entrance, and into a place that resembled the accident ward of a hospital. There was a desk and a warder writing in a large book, a weighing scales, a device for measuring height, and bath cubicles.

'This fellow's dabs are wanted in a hurry, Mick,' said the warder, indicating the boy.

The boy looked at him rather anxiously.

'I can't do fifty things at once,' said Mick, from the desk. 'I can't take him up to have his dabs done and attend to these other fellows at the one time.'

'Well I thought I could take him up while you fixed up the others.'

'Right so, take him away, the rest get ready for a bath. Stab-the-Rasher!'

A fat prisoner came round the cubicle, carrying a towel over his arm.

'Well?' he said.

'Don't "well" me. Take these fellows and show them each a cubicle. Nine inches of water apiece, and a sup extra for Tralee Trembles here. Throw a sup of Lysol into his, too, and take care he doesn't drink it.' To the other warder: 'I'll fix up with the Guard here, too, while you're away. Give us their property, Guard.'

The Guard gave him the envelopes out of his satchel, and the boy went off with the other warder.

They went out into the yard and through the main entrance.

They passed principal warders with harps on their sleeves, and each time they did, the warder saluted. They stopped at a door and waited.

'Does it—does it hurt, sir?' asked the boy anxiously.

'No talking!' said the warder, and knocked again. 'Might as well go in and wait.'

They went into a room furnished with a counter and a trayful of printed forms.

'What do you mean,' said the warder when they had closed the door behind them, 'by starting a conversation with me out there, and the corridor rotten with governors, chiefs, principals, clerks, and the devil knows what?'

'I'm sorry, sir,' said the boy, near to tears, 'but I didn't know. I was never in prison before.'

'And time enough if you were never in it. What were you saying, anyway?'

'I was only asking, sir, if it hurt—if it hurt much, I mean?'

'If what hurt?'

'Having me—whatever he said——'

'Having your dabs taken?' said the warder, smiling. 'Of course it doesn't hurt, you little eedgit. It's only what they call on the pictures your fingerprints. The Guards want them in a hurry, and your ould fellow, or whoever looks after you, must have refused to have it done in the Bridewell, so they had to shift you up here to do it. Your ould fellow was a sensible man, because I bet they shifted you up here on the double then. If you were only picked last night, they might have left you the weekend in the Bridewell. Here, bad as it is, you'll get a bed and enough of food and a walk around the yard anyway.'

The boy began to say something but the door was opening, and the warder gave him a stern look.

Another warder came in, carrying a tray containing a bar of copper, a roller, and a container of printing ink.

'This him?' he said to the warder. 'Right, are your hands clean?' The boy showed his hands. 'They'll do.' He took a form and laid it on the counter and rolled ink on the bar.

'Index finger. No, that one.' He took it and inked it— 'Don't press, I'll do that'—and rolled it on the form, where

31

it left an impression in the space marked 'Index Finger,' in the half of the form marked, 'Right Hand.' 'Now, middle finger; right, now ring finger; no this one, the next one, you lugawn. Right, the little finger. Now, very good, more ink. The left hand. Index, middle, ring, and left. Very good. Now, can you write your name?'

'Yes sir, certainly, sir.'

'Well write it on the bottom, in that space there.'

In big childish letters, the boy wrote: 'Frank Mulvany.'

'Should I have put Kevin, too, sir? It's me confirmation name.'

'No, that'll do all right, the cops know enough about you.'

The boy gave a little smile and went back with the warder to the reception.

The others were standing already washed and with pillow-slips under their arms containing sheets and a towel.

'It'll be a nuisance giving him a bath on his own,' said Mick, at his desk.

'Sure won't he be getting a bath anyway with the Juveniles on Monday?'

'Could you last out till Monday, young fellow? I know you were never in your life before as long as three whole days without a bath.'

The boy laughed, relieved, because he didn't fancy taking off his clothes before all these old fellows and because the warder had made a joke.

'Right,' said Mick, 'to the dungeons. Take them away.'

They marched in single file through the main corridor, and into the prison.

'Halt; stand here in the centre and no talking.'

The circle seemed to be the main street of the prison. It was at the junction of the four wings: *A* leading straight west, *B* and *C* at angles in the middle, and *D* the continuation of *A* going east. There were steel galleries all round, three of them in each wing, and steel stairs, joining them.

Beside *A* wing was the shaft to the kitchen, and beside them, in the centre of the circle, was a stone pillar with a triangle hanging on it.

The boy followed their gaze towards the bottom of *D* wing, where there was a red metal door with a barred gate, painted aluminium, over it.

'That's the door of the hang-house,' said one of the prisoners.

'I know,' said Tralee Trembles. 'We used to call it the dance-hall.'

6

THE warder spoke to a principal and turned to the prisoners.

'Right, follow me.' He led them down *B* wing to a staircase in the middle and told them to go below in front of him.

On the turn of the stairs the maintenance man turned to the boy. 'We're going to the Base, but we'll only be here till after dinner. Then we'll be brought up here to our cells. You'll go over to the Juveniles.'

They halted in a dark passage, lit by a single bulb.

'Stand to a cell door each of you,' shouted a warder.

The boy, reluctant to move from the others, walked slowly.

'Come on you,' shouted the warder, 'get a move on yourself there.'

He opened doors and each man went into a cell. The boy was last.

'Come on you,' said the warder, almost throwing him into the cell. 'Get in there.'

The door was banged and the boy looked round. Only half of the window was above the level of the ground. It looked out into a sort of trench. On the walls were inscriptions.

'Dear mother, sell the pig and buy me out.'

Under this another hand had written : 'Pig dead, soldier

on. James P. McGinn took a lady's watch to mind it safe. 3 years P.S.'

There were lovers' hearts and prayers and a few drawings; the boy examined them all with interest. Then he sat on the stool and looked at the floor and thought what he would do with that warder if he saw him outside. He'd give him pushing and shoving and roaring and bawling! But he'd never be outside again : and he gave a long, long sniff and turned it into a sneeze—or was trying to, when the door opened.

'Here, come on, jump to it.' The warder was standing beside a prisoner, and the prisoner was carrying a tray with aluminium cans on it. It was the dinner.

'Take one, can't you?' said the warder.

The boy took one, and the warder, muttering, 'Don't know what's up with the youth going nowadays. When I was your age I used to meet meself coming back,' banged the door.

The container on top held potatoes, and in the can there was a thick soup. The boy had a plate and a spoon, and even salt, on the table. Before the warder had banged the last of the doors, he had the lot eaten.

The warder was outside his cell again. 'I'll give it to him,' he said.

Oh, God, what was it for this time? The door was opened.

'Hey, you,' shouted the warder in at him. 'Sleep in your skin, come on, can't you?'

He was holding a container. 'Could you go a few more spuds?'

The boy nodded eagerly.

'With the compliments of Tralee Trembles.' The boy took them and smiled his thanks. 'He's a Food Pioneer.' The warder banged the door.

The boy ate the potatoes and felt better in a lot of ways. That old warder was dead witty. Real quick off his mark.

He smiled to himself, thinking of the warder's jokes.

Over in the hospital they were getting dinner. A prisoner was taking it round to the cells. Some prisoners were standing at their doors, but there were some in bed.

One of these asked the orderly to bring his in and put it on the stool beside his bed. He spoke in an English accent.

'That Limey,' said the prisoner to the warder. 'Does he think I'm his servant or something?'

'Oh, what odds!' said the warder. 'He won't be with us that long. They're anxious to get him over in his own place.'

'Good riddance and all,' said the prisoner, bringing in a can of food to the bedside. 'Hey you, Limey. Why can't you get up and take it at the door like anyone else? You're not dead, you know.'

'Be a good chap and fetch me some water, will you?'

The prisoner breathed heavily and spoke to the warder. 'He wants me to get him water, now.' He shouted back into the cell: 'Are you sure, my lord, you wouldn't like a bottle of wine? I'm just going down to the cellar.'

'Get him the water,' said the warder. 'I'll get Cairnes to help me with the rest of the dinners.'

'I hope you get this service on the "Moor" when you're doing your ten stretch,' said the prisoner, taking up Limey's jug and going to the recess. The warder called another prisoner and went on with the dinners.

When he came back, the prisoner spoke in low tones. 'Listen, Limey, the Scarperer is sending up a man today to visit me. Now, he'll want definite word. About if you're sure you've got that five thousand nicker to pay him with, if he takes you out? Because, I'm telling you, breaking out of this place is a puddin' compared to getting offside from the Scarperer, if you try to work a stroke on him.'

'My dear man, you're becoming tiresome on the subject. It's worth it to me. If I'm taken back to England, I'm liable

36

to about a ten stretch; apart from that, under the 'Forty-nine Act, three times up the steps, Assizes or Sessions, and you can be sent to Preventative Detention for the rest of your natural. I'd die on the Isle of Sheppey. They'd just throw away the key.'

'I know you've a lot of form and I know what you'd get, but have you the readies outside? The Scarperer isn't the Scarlet bloody Pimpernel, you know. He doesn't pull these strokes from the goodness of his heart. He reckons on one of these jobs to keep him going for about two years. With a bit of fiddling in between times, of course.'

'Well, supposing I ask you something. What about this old bloke we're playing dummy with? He hasn't appeared yet.'

'He's in the Base. He'll be over today. One of the blokes came over for a dose of medicine and told me he'd seen him in the circle.'

'I see.'

'Nick, here's the screw back. I'll tell them it'll be all right, then?'

'Right as the mail, Jerry, and the gelt is as safe as the Bank of England.'

'Synnott, receptions,' shouted the warder, outside.

'Here's our dummy,' said Jerry, then, raising his voice, 'and the next time you get up like anyone else!'

'I only asked you to walk a few yards with my food.'

'Next time I'll throw it over you.'

The warder came up to the door. 'Come on, Jerry. I want to get this reception through and locked up, and you want your dinner. Don't be minding this fellow. We won't be troubled with him much longer.'

'How right you are!' murmured Limey, as the door shut on him.

Tralee stood in the corridor.

'Here you are now,' said the warder, 'this man will show you your cell.'

On the way Jerry asked him: 'Would you like a ball of malt in the morning? A real genuine Baby Power?'[1]

'Would a duck swim?' asked Tralee.

'Well, there's a fellow here is mad for aspirins. He can only get two at a time. You ask for some yourself in the morning and bring them to this cell door, here.'

'He must be a funny class of a man would give a glass of whiskey for a couple of ould aspirins.'

'He's an Englishman,' said Jerry Synnott.

'Oh,' said Tralee, as if that explained it.

1. John Powers whiskey

7

JERRY, as hospital orderly, had the privilege of eating his dinner in company. In the kitchen, with the cooks. Sometimes the warder on duty would have a bite with them, for they dined by no means poorly. Caviare they had not, nor peacocks' ears in aspic, but spuds and cabbage and the best of meat. For the hospital got the best of the meat that came into the prison, and the cooks the best of the meat that came into the hospital; for, as the saying has it, first up is the best dressed.

They ate in silence, till the tea was served. The warder absent-mindedly let a cigarette fall beside each plate, and the others got them to their mouths without ill-bred comment on either side.

'Jerry,' said the warder. 'You better get a tie on as soon as we collect the diet cans from the cells. There's a visit for you, this afternoon.'

'I've had my visit at the beginning of the month, and I didn't put in for a special one. It can't be me.'

'It is you,' said the warder, 'it has your name on the form. Think I can't read properly or something?'

'Certainly,' said the cook, a fat jovial man like a cook out of a film, doing twelve months for Grievous Bodily. 'We all knows a man in your position has to be educated. No one is ever made a screw, barrin' he's been at Trinity College.'

'A lot you'd know about Trinity College, or any other college,' said the warder sourly.

'I was through it, if you want to know,' said the cook. 'Myself and Dimples Daly. Only we were caught coming out the Lincoln Place gate with our athletic trophies, what we'd won be climbing up down-spouts.'

'It's a wonder you didn't become a screw yourself, so,' said the warder.

'Well, I nearly was,' said the cook, 'only for I was disqualified at the last minute. Be the reason of the facts being that they discovered I was a baptised Christian.'

'Listen,' said Jerry, before the warder could carry on the discussion. 'Shut up a minute, till I find out about this visit. You don't know who it is, is coming to visit me?'

'I do,' said the warder. 'It's a gentleman from the Society for the Rehabilitation of Recidivist Prisoners.'

'The old lags' home, like,' said the cook.

'They go in for lags that have a lot of form,' said the warder, 'and you must have put your name down with the chaplain.'

'I didn't.'

'Well, they must have heard about you from somewhere. This gentleman is after getting permission from the Department to come up here today. He says it's about a job.'

'A screwing job more than likely,' said the cook. 'Some rockery round Grafton Street he has cased.'

Jerry turned an angry look on the cook and barely winked. 'Shut up a minute, can't you.' He seemed to think that the cook's comment, for some reason, was in bad taste.

'Only an eedgit would mind that eedgit,' said the warder consolingly. 'It'll do you no harm anyway to see the gentleman. Sure, if nothing else, you might put the arm on him for a few quid.'

'That's right,' said the cook, 'he has experience at that. The time he got the five stretch for armed begging.'

'I'll go out, anyway, and see him,' said Jerry.

40

'And make sure, avic,' said the cook, 'you've washed up after our dying comrades above, before you go out, or the crockery will be waiting on you here, when you come back.'

'Jerry doesn't have to be told his work be the likes of you,' said the warder. 'Besides, you only have to do the washing up for the ones that are in bed.'

'Except that Limey,' said Jerry. 'There's nothing the matter with him, that he can't do his own.'

'Ah, sure, what odds is it?' said the screw. 'If he's in bed, he's in bed, and it's the doctor you want to complain to, not me. He's complaining of his nerves.'

'That's right,' said the cook. 'Lord Goddard keeps appearing to him in his sleep. To welcome him back to dear old Blighty.'

'There's the two o'clock bell,' said the warder, 'go on up, Jerry, and get your washing up done, and then you can have a shave and put your tie on and be ready for this visit.'

The usual Saturday afternoon visits were in progress in the boxes. Prisoners sat in compartments like those of a discreet pawnshop, and talked across a counter to their relatives or friends in the opposite compartment. A warder supervised the proceedings, walking up and down the space between them, consulting his watch now and then and warning each prisoner when his time was up, and signing a form for his assistant to pass the departing visitor through the gates.

Jerry, however, was brought to a small room, reserved for business visits, and was told to wait till his visitor was passed in from the gate.

'Right, Mr. Coldwell. You're the visitor for Synnott? In here, please.'

'You're Jeremiah Synnott?' asked Mr. Coldwell. He was a well-dressed man with a black moustache and in morning clothes. 'Just the dress for a formal call, eh, Officer?' He smiled at the warder. 'I've just come from a wedding.'

41

'What harm, sir? It's not often indeed we see the like up here. Don't mind me, sir. I'm sure anything you have to tell Synnott will be for his good. I'm just making up a few entries here in me book.' The warder bent over his writing in the far end of the room and then went to the door and spoke to the warder in the other compartment.

'I like the get-up, Eddie,' said Jerry in low tones.

'Burkes of Dame Street,' said Mr. Collins, for he it was. 'The moustache is my own. I carry it with my shirts. That all right? Did Limey say the gelt was OK and the dummy arrived all right?'

'Just come over from the Base, and Limey says the dough is as safe as a house.'

'I see,' said Eddie Collins, in a loud tone. 'Well, my man, as you say, you have some two years to do, even if you get your full remission and a job.'

'Ah, he's a puddin' to get that, sir,' said the warder, looking up. 'Never gives a bit of trouble, Jerry doesn't. Very helpful.'

'I hope you will repay the confidence of the staff in you, Synnott.'

'Ah, I'm sure he will, sir.'

'But at the moment, it's a bit premature discussing plans for your future employment. However, I'll make a note of your case.' He wrote in an official-looking notebook stamped 'Society for the Rehabilitation of Recidivist Prisoners.'

'Where the hell did you get your hands on that?' asked Jerry from the side of his mouth.

'Honestly obtained, with hard-pinched money,' said Eddie Collins. 'Ten guineas subscription. I'm a life-member.' Then, in the loud tone: 'I see, Synnott, most interesting. I can see you're not a bad type at heart. We'll continue to take an interest in your case. On the double,' he said in a lower tone, and while he spoke the next sentence, Jerry also spoke.

42

'Out at the first brewery bell,' said Eddie Collins, 'down the canal and to the garage at the second.'

'And we'll have the dummy parcelled up and dumped and all, by that time,' said Jerry. 'I promised him a glass of malt if he'd bring two aspirins over to your man's cell in the morning.'

'And the bars are nearly cut through and all.' Mr. Collins smiled again and said loudly: 'You know, there's a lot of good in you, Synnott.'

'Out at the first brewery bell and down to the garage at the second,' Jerry repeated. 'Thank you, sir. I understand everything, sir, and I won't let you down, sir.'

'And see that you don't let the gentleman down,' said the warder from the far end of the box. And, to Mr. Collins: 'If you're ready, sir, I'll take you to the gate.'

8

AT TWELVE o'clock the night patrol met in the circle. The men on it were Tiny Teevan, a Tyrone man, six feet, three inches in his stockinged feet, and Donlan, a small wiry Limerick man.

The principal gave them their beats.

'You will take, in turn, all wings and the hospital. Donlan will do *A* wing and *B* wing, and you, Teevan, will do *C* wing and *D* wing.'

Teevan gulped. 'All *D* wing, sir?'

'Of course. What's the matter with you, man?'

'It's the way,' said Donlan, 'it's the way he doesn't like going to the bottom of it, sir, at night-time.'

'He what . . . ?'

'There's that old red door on the . . . the . . .' said Teevan, opening wide his big blue eyes.

'That what? The hang-house?' asked the principal.

'I do hear quare things, sir, at night-time down that part of the buildings,' said Teevan, miserably. 'And, sir, you know me. From the time we were in the Crumlin together, sir, when we were lads, sir, before the change-over.'

'I do,' said the principal, 'I remember you well, Teevan.' He turned to Donlan. 'I saw him with his cap perched on the back of his head, like some fellow was delivering messages for the railway, and old Johnson, the chief, asked him in God's name could he not fix his cap straight like anyone else? He looked at the chief and says he, "I can't, sur, fur it's too wee, sur," and Johnson looked at him for a minute, like a duck looking at thunder, and then offered, with whatever voice was left him, to pay your man's fare back to Tyrone among the bushes.'

Teevan chuckled deeply at this, 'He did, sir, he did that.'

'And what the hell brought him down here to persecute us for another thirty-odd years is more nor I can fathom.'

'It was the fishing, sir, that and I knew me wife wouldn't come down to the Free State. She never did like Fenians, sir,' he added frankly. 'A bitter woman any way you took her. I never minded the poor creatures. Whatever harm was in them, it's only their ignorance. When all is said and done, sir, yiz are only poor dumb bastes like ourselves.'

'Thanks, Teevan,' said the principal, 'it's more nor civil of you.'

'Don't mention it, sir,' said Teevan. 'Everyone can't be born into enlightenment.'

'Well, neither this nor that, but D wing is to be patrolled like anywhere else. Maybe you'll take the other side, then, Teevan. If you don't mind passing the door of the work-shop, in case a ghostly hand would drag you and put you to work on one of the looms.'

'I don't mind taking the other side, sir,' said Donlan.

'Right. Off with you,' said the principal. 'Good-night, I'm off. I hope you don't meet nothing worse than yourself, Tiny.'

'Thanks, sir,' said Teevan, 'you're more nor decent.'

'I got the half-dozen, Dan,' said Teevan in a whisper.

'And I got the two one-and-ones and a bit of salt an' vinegar,' said Donlan.

'We'll go into the doctor's room and have a bit of a feed and a chat.'

'About ghosts.'

'Don't say the like, Dan. I dreamt of herself last night,

and it's not lucky. We see then, but in a glass darkly.'

'That's all right, Tiny,' said Donlan. 'I whipped two tumblers the other night, above in the Hut when the curate wasn't looking.'

They opened their packages of chips, laid out the salt and vinegar, while Tiny felt in his pocket for a corkscrew and Donlan put out the glasses.

'. . . so I says to him, says I,' said Teevan, 'there's only three things to worry Civil Servants the likes of us, me dear man, and them's the three P's—Pay, Promotion, and Pension. Wasn't I right, Dan?'

'You were all that,' said Donlan, 'and I think it's time now we went round and had a look in at these fellows to see they haven't cut their throats in the night.'

'Heaven forgive you, Dan, for thinking the like! I'll be imagining that, and I putting on the light and looking in the spy-hole. You're a terrible man to put it into me head, and I just digesting me few chips and me bit of fish and the couple of bottles.'

'That reminds me to put away the empties,' said Donlan, taking down a heavy volume from a shelf, entitled *Statutory Rules and Standing Orders re the Treatment of Sick Prisoners. Section III: Notes on Judicial Executions.*

He placed the bottles and glasses in the space behind and put back the book. 'That's where the medical orderly hides his own,' he said, straightening his tunic and wiping his mouth. 'You take from the workshop back, and I'll start from the bottom of *D* wing. If I don't come back to meet you in the circle, you'll know I was grabbed be the ghost of Lynchehaun.'

'I thought he got away with life.'

'So he did. He was in cell A, I, 5, just where you're going now as you turn the corner.'

'Oh, 'scurse you!' said Tiny, flitting heavily down the passage and turning on lights and looking into cells, as if

46

every sleeping prisoner he looked in at was chief exhibit in the Chamber of Horrors.

They met again later on.

'Well,' said Donlan, 'that doesn't seem to be a bad class of a morning.' They were walking across the yard to the hospital. 'We'll go in here, open up the cook, lock him in the kitchen till the day man comes on, and we've another fellow to open, too: Synnott, one of the orderlies. He's going into the store to check some kit, and have it ready for the steward's inspection today. The screw would have had to come in early, only he volunteered.'

'Wasn't that the decent man?' said Teevan.

'He was, though I've no doubt there was a bit of snout hanging on the job. I wouldn't mind that, though, I'd swap twenty Afton[1] for a lie in bed any day of the week.'

The cook was got up, muttering and cursing, but the orderly was ready dressed and waiting for them when they opened the door. Donlan took him to the store and locked him up and left the hospital with Teevan.

Jerry waited with his ear to the door of the stores, which was a converted cell, till they closed the outer gate after them. From the piles of sheets, underwear and clothes, he made a bundle that obscured a view of the window from the spy-hole, stuffed the sides of the door with clothes, and, in his soundproof chamber, went to work.

The window was a full-length hospital window, not the usual cell window set high in the wall. He drew a hacksaw blade set in a piece of wood from the middle of a pile of sheets, scraped out a filling of iron filings, dust and spit, from the cross-cut in the first of the bars, and quickly sawed through to the finish. He replaced the filling and went to work on the second, on which less progress had been made on previous stints.

As the signal for half-past seven went, he replaced the

1. Cigarettes

47

sheets and underwear before the warder opened the door.

'Got it all done, Jerry?'

'Yes. We're only short two pillow-slips and a pair of Robert Emmets. We can make that up from the Reception. We'll go over the list at dinner-time.'

'Good lad. I'll open them up for slopping out and then you can go down and get a cup of tea.'

'That reminds me. The Limey wants to stay in bed and wants no breakfast. His lordship doesn't want to be disturbed till the doctor comes around.'

'There, I told you. There might be something wrong with the poor devil.'

'And that new fellow———'

'Tralee Trembles.'

'He wants aspirins.'

'He can come over to me now, while you're fixing up the others. Just bang out the Englishman's door when he's slopped out and leave him so, will you? I'll go in now and get me applications done. I've opened them up, and you can send Tralee over to the office.'

Jerry removed a bottle with a rag stopper from under the linen and went to Limey's cell.

'Right,' said Limey, jumping up fully dressed and standing behind the door.

'Here,' Tralee whispered, holding aspirin in his palm. 'He gave me four.'

'OK,' said Jerry. 'Come in here a minute.'

'Where's the whiskey?' asked Tralee.

'Here,' said Jerry, catching him by the hair and forcing the soaked rag over his nose.

Tralee went limp and they dumped him into the bed and pulled the clothes over his head, carefully placing his bare arm over the blanket.

'Quick,' said Jerry, 'down to the store.'

They went in and locked the door after them.

9

IN THE store Jerry moved the sheets and underwear against the door, obscuring the view of the window from the spy-hole. He went to the window and twisted the bars, the filling of iron filings and spit falling out of the cuts as he did so.

He and Limey climbed through and stood a couple of yards from the wall, their backs against the window.

'Stand off the cabbage,' he whispered to Limey.

'Oh,' said Limey, 'I hadn't noticed.' He looked down between his feet. 'Big, isn't it, for the time of year?'

' 'Morning all,' murmured a voice from the top of the wall.

'You, too, Lugs,' said Jerry, 'make haste and let down that rope.'

'All in good time.' He sat astride the wall, unhooked the coils of a rope ladder, and fixed it to the wall. They quickly climbed up and sat on the wall, either side of Lugs. He drew up the rope and turned the hooks so that it hung down the other side. They climbed down and he followed.

'Down like the hammers of hell, along the canal bank and down to Binn's Bridge. Eddie has the van waiting there at the garage. I'll get down the rope and go home in the bus.'

Getting his breath, Jerry said: 'The Scarperer is very economical with his business equipment.'

'It's not that,' said Lugs, reaching up with a long fishing rod for the hooks, 'but we don't want the screws to see or know anything till that old man comes out of the chloroform.'

A factory siren sounded a few bridges down the canal.

'That's it,' said Jerry, 'we're to be down there on the second one. Let's get moving, Limey. Thanks, Lugs.'

'That's all right, Jerry, you can do the same for me sometime.'

They went down the canal bank, and, when their breath was equal to it, broke into a run.

Lugs was having a conversation with himself.

'Seems a pity about that nice fishing rod. I think I'll just leave it on the bank instead of throwing it away. Maybe some kid will find it. Bet it cost a right few nicker and all. But, here'—he coiled the rope ladder round a large stone, and flung it far from him, into the water, wiped his hands and walked up towards Cross Guns Bridge for the bus back into the city.

A man walking greyhounds passed him on the bank and nodded. 'Nice morning.'

Lugs removed his hat and remarked with jovial warmth, 'It's all that, sir, if we had anything to go with it.'

Eddie was waiting at the garage with the van.

'A gallon, sir, that right?' asked the attendant.

'That's it,' said Eddie Collins, looking at his watch, 'and see how the tyres are, will you?'

The attendant walked round the van.

'They're all right, sir.'

'Oil?'

'I've already given it, sir.'

50

'Well, wait now. There was something.'

'By the way, sir, the doors at the back are open, sir.'

'Oh, yes, I know. Leave them as they are. It's for ventilation, you know.'

A second factory siren sounded, farther along the canal.

'I see, sir,' said the attendant, doubtfully.

'That's for ten past eight, is it?'

'Yes, sir. We'll be getting a regular queue now, sir. On their way into town.'

'Mournful sound that horn, hasn't it?'

'It's from Mountjoy, sir. Not the prison, the brewery.'

'The prison? Oh, yes. I've heard of it. "In Mountjoy one Monday morning," and all that.'

'Yes, sir.'

'Funny name for a prison. Though there is a prison in Paris called La Santé. It means "health." '

'Yes, sir.'

Eddie looked in his mirror and said: 'Go over and get me a paper from that fellow there.' He produced a pound note. 'Get me all the morning papers.'

'Certainly, sir,' said the attendant, going across the road.

Jerry and the Limey came round the corner from the canal bank.

Eddie put the van into gear, and said turning round: 'Bang the doors.'

They settled themselves in the van and banged over the doors. 'Right, Ned,' said Jerry.

The van swung out on the road gathering speed as it turned the corner of Belvedere Road, narrowly missing the garage attendant, who came running across with the papers.

'Your papers, sir . . . your change.'

Eddie waved his hand and shouted, 'Keep it,' and the van raced over the North Circular Road with Eddie's hand tight on the horn.

51

Two boys were at the canal bank:

'Come on,' said Yammin (spelt Eamonn) McLough-lin. 'Hurry up, it's after half-eight. And I don't want to be belted when I get in. I was late two days last week and Juicy Jaws promised me what he'd give me, if I didn't get in in time.'

'You must have forgotten,' said Shaybo Keenan, 'it's students we have today. They begin this week.'

'That's right,' said Yammin. 'I forgot that.'

They surveyed the bottom of the canal at their ease.

'No pinkeens out yet,' said Yammin. 'They must only get born in the warm weather.'

'But there's a dead dog down here,' said Shaybo, farther down the canal.

'And look, what I see——'

'Me, too,' said Shaybo, also grabbing for the fishing rod.

'I saw it first.'

'I got it first. It's a dinger, ain't it?'

'It is, and it's mine.'

'Well, I'll tell you what we'll do. It separates; we'll half it and toss up for the end with the line.'

'No, we'll sell it. To old Teevan. He's mad about fishing and he'll give us a few bob for it. Maybe,' breathlessly, 'maybe he'll give us—five bob for it.'

'A half-a-dollar each.'

'We'll dump it here in the bushes, in case someone sees it and lifts it on us.'

'And get it on our way back to the quarters at lunch hour.'

'Old Teevan is on nights, but he'll be out of bed then. Let's hurry down to school now.'

Quite a crowd had collected and Yammin stopped in his tracks, touching Shaybo on the arm as he did so.

'Ah, wait your hour. It's only the students,' said Shaybo. But he was wrong. The student, a pale and nervous young man, was there, but their own master, Juicy Jaws, was there also, with a stout Christian Brother taking the overflow of boys who presumed to come late because it was. the students' week.

But rubbing their hands, they consoled themselves, thinking of the fishing rod and what old Teevan would give them for it.

At eleven o'clock the hospital warder was running round looking for Tralee Trembles.

'The doctor is on his way over, and one of my receptions. is missing. Where can he have got himself to?'

'Maybe he's scarpered,' said the cook facetiously.

'He hadn't the strength to walk, not to mind get over the wall,' said the warder, 'but we'll all live to be old. Oh, here's the doctor. Cook, get round and get Tralee to the doctor's door; I'll open up this other fellow.' He opened Limey's door, and drew back the bed-clothes. 'Come on, wake up; the doctor's here to see you.'

His jaw dropped, 'Tralee, it's Tralee. It's . . . he's . . . he's . . .' He put his hand inside the old man's shirt. 'Cook, quick, quick, get the doctor. Quick, quick, and tell him to. hurry.'

He reached over and pressed a bell, and another warder came in.

'Hurry and sound the alarm. Limey is scarpered. He's. away, gone over the wall.'

All over the North Side of the city the siren moaned and warders came dashing in from the quarters, except Teevan, who was playing a trout, from one side of the bed to the other.

10

THE medical orderly came out of the Limey's cell. 'Here,' said the principal. 'Get them all locked up. Or,' with heavy sarcasm, 'as many as you have left!'

'The doctor is in with Tralee—with James Guiney, sir, and I'm——'

'Never mind that now, the doctor can attend to that. Go round, you, and get them into their cells.'

'I'll get the crowd out of the kitchen first.' The medical orderly spoke in a daze.

'Go down and get them then; don't stand there like an ass at the Horse Show. Get them up and into their cells.'

'Yes, sir, certainly, sir.' The medical orderly hurried down to the kitchen. 'Come on up,' he shouted, 'and get into your cells. Let me count you.'

'Count me, so,' said the cook. 'You'll find I add up to one. At least I did the last time I was counted.' He was annoyed, having just wet a pot of tea for himself and his assistant. 'Doran is down there in the scullery, peeling spuds. You can count him when he comes up.'

'Doran,' said the medical orderly, 'come up here.'

Doran came up, wiping his hands on his apron.

'Fall in there,' said the medical orderly.

'He adds up to one, too,' said the cook. 'It's a pity we're not centipedes or maggots that you could cut in two and make more out of, but we're only Irishmen and it takes two of us to make a pair.'

'One, two,' said the medical orderly.

'That's right. You got the answer first time.'

'Into your cells and shut out the door.' He looked round at the principal. 'Two, all correct, sir.'

'Have you checked the rest of them?'

'Five in bed, sir.'

'And your own orderly?'

'That's Jerry. Where—oh, yes, I know.'

'You know! What do you know?'

'I know where he is, sir.'

'Well, that's something. You don't know where this English fellow is, do you? Well, I'll tell you where he is. He's gone over that wall. That's what he's done. That's where he is.'

'He's in doing the sheets and underclothes—I mean Jerry is. In here, sir.'

He opened the door of the store. 'Jerry, Jerry, come on.' He shoved over the pile of clothes. 'Jerry!'

His eyes travelled to the window. He gulped and turned miserably from the door. 'I don't know, I did know . . . he was here this morning . . . the window, the bars.'

The principal swelled in the face, cursed with what breath he could command, and pushing the medical orderly aside, looked in at the store and at the broken bars.

'Ah!' He clapped his hands to his head and asked quietly: 'You're not giving them their annual leave in pairs, are you?'

Then he shouted: 'Come up here, one of you, and dash over and get on that phone. Say there's another one scarpered, Synnott. How do I know his number? Get it from the card. You!' he shouted at the medical orderly. 'Get out there, with the rest of them and search—the grounds, the land, the potato field,' and with a tragic yell that was almost a shriek: 'Don't let the pigs out!'

'I wouldn't mind,' said the medical orderly to himself, 'but he promised to have all that kit ready counted for the

55

steward when he'd come round. Very deceitful.' And he shook his head.

'. . . Yes this is the Detective Division, Lower Castle Yard. Two men escaped. You're the Chief Warder. Yes, you've notified Mountjoy Garda Station. Yes, I've got that. We've identified him. Just got word from Scotland Yard, thanking us and telling us they were sending over for him. I'll tell them they needn't bother, and when we do get them back, we'll send him over direct. They might take better care of him over there. That's all right, the message came through from the local station, a while ago. By the way, have you far to go from the phone back to the office? No? Only a few yards? Well, don't lose yourself on the way back. And tell them up there, we don't mind no, it keeps us going. You're shocking decent, letting them out like that. Provides employment. Oh, don't mention it.' He hung up the phone.

'Superintendent, Special Branch, to speak to the assistant commissioner. You're through, sir.'

'Good morning, Superintendent.'

' 'Morning, sir. It's about James Kirke.'

'Oh, yes. They've definitely identified him in London, haven't they? The commissioner spoke to me from Scotland Yard last night. He was most complimentary. I made a note of the officers responsible for the arrest. I felt like telling the commissioner that they were two years looking for him, and he was only a few days here when we picked him up. But I don't like to rub it in. He was very grateful when I told him we had him.'

'*Had* him is right, sir.'

'What do you mean, Superintendent? He was identified from his fingerprints, was he not?'

'Oh, the dabs were all right, sir. We had him all right. But we haven't him now, sir. We've lost him. At least, the crowd up above have. He broke out of the 'Joy this morn-

56

ing, sir. Himself and another fellow. Irishman by the name of Jeremiah Synnott.'

'Did you get through to London?'

'Not yet, sir. You told me yesterday you were ringing them yourself about this matter. You'd be speaking to the commissioner there this morning about it.'

'But that was before I knew—I mean—er, ring them yourself this morning, Superintendent, and tell them to make my apologies to the commissioner. You can say I'm not feeling too well this morning.'

'And that,' said the assistant commissioner, 'is the gospel truth.'

'. . . Jeremiah Synnott, aged twenty-nine; weight eleven stone, eyes grey, wearing prison clothes. Dublin accent. . . .'

'. . . James Kirke, alias Eric James Watts, aged forty-eight; height five feet nine, weight twelve stone two, eyes brown, hair bald on top. London accent, well-spoken. Both criminal records. Same issued on separate sheet, not for Garda public notices. All right.'

'Special blocks, black frame, front-page photos as in Garda public notice. That's it. Good luck, Mick.'

'Good luck, Paddy. And it's to go over to London straight away.'

'That's all right. *Hue and Cry* will have the blocks and copy by tomorrow's plane.'

The Scarperer leaned over the table and examined a poster with interest. It was in French: 'AVIS!' And in larger lettering: 'ATTENTION!' It was an official poster of the Sûreté Nationale and announced that they and the Préfecture were anxious to get their hands on the robber and assassin whose photograph took up half the space on the poster. The face bore a marked resemblance to Limey's—alias Eric James Watts, alias James Kirke.

Eddie Collins entered the room, holding a similar police

notice in his hands, but this one was headed 'GARDA SIOCHANA.'

'Just got it in the post office. Gave the kid half a dollar for it.'

'Thanks, Eddie,' said the Scarperer, 'leave it down beside this other one.'

They put the posters side by side and studied them.

'That's in French,' said Eddie. 'I didn't know he was wanted there, too!'

'He's not. Never been there, so far as I know,' said the Scarperer.

'Well, what do you think they have his mush on a police poster for, then?'

'That's not his face. That's a client of ours in Paris called Pierre le Fou—Peter the Mad One. Though the only mad thing I know about him is that he's mad with villainy.'

'Well, he's certainly a dead ringer for the Limey.'

'He'd be very pleased to hear you say that. I'm sending him the two posters by Collinstown tonight, so as he'll see for himself. You take them out to that fellow you know, and tell him to dump them in the Mabillon, Boulevard Saint-Germain, the corner of the rue de Buci——'

'To be called for be Jeeny et All, spelt "Genie Etoile." I know. He thinks it's about Sweep tickets.'

II

AT HALF past seven a new Customline swung out through the Castle gates and down Dame Street.

'Which way now, Sergeant?' asked the driver.

'I suppose Spillane's of Gardiner Street might be worth a visit. Well begun is half done. We can work back from the North Side.'

'Across O'Connell Bridge, down Eden Quay, across Beresford Place and up into Lower Gardiner Street. I suppose that would be the best way.'

'Certainly,' said a middle-aged detective, sitting in the back with the sergeant, 'if you want everyone the whole length and breadth of the district to know that we're on our way there.'

The sergeant clucked his tongue and said to the middle-aged man: 'You're right, Mick. Don't you think he'd have thought of that himself, without you or me having to tell him?'

The middle-aged man and the sergeant hated each other like poison because of the sergeant's promotion and some other squabbles that they would have described as 'politics.' They were, therefore, always very polite to each other and showed it by abusing lesser policemen when they were together, which broke the monotony of their abuse of each other when they were apart.

The car had reached Westmoreland Street and the driver

was afraid to make the slightest suggestion in case they would fall on him again.

'Which way, now, ah?' he said nervously, lapsing into his native accent.

'Take it this way, avic,' said the sergeant soothingly. Like Lanna Machree's dog, he liked to go a bit of the road with everyone. 'Go up straight to Dorset Street and we'll turn right, and to the top of Upper Gardiner Street and down on top of them from that direction. Taking them unawares, as you'd say.'

'I see that fellow Cole on the pavement there,' said the middle-aged man. 'There above Findlater's Church. Fellow used to be a warder above there.'

'You've an eye like a hawk,' said the sergeant, admiringly, 'I see him there. Looking in the garage window That fellow made a right few ha'pence up there, shopping in drink and cigarettes and shopping out letters; and the last night before he was given his notice, bringing the files and dumping the ladder for that other pair to scarper a couple of years ago.'

'Will I go in on the kerb for him?' asked the driver eagerly.

The sergeant and the detective looked at each other hopelessly and clicked their tongues in unison.

'Ah, she's rearing them yet,' said the detective.

'Well, dear knows,' said the sergeant frankly, 'you'll never get your promotion, acting that stupid. Am I right, Mick?'

'I suppose you are,' said Mick, who felt it was a bit of a dig, as the man said, at himself.

'But I mean to say,' said the sergeant. 'That's all right, go right here and wait on the lights. We're no more than anyone else, now, down Dorset Street. If we wanted to tell everyone we're out to find out whatever we can about this fellow breaking out of the 'Joy this morning, not to mention his confederate, we'd pull in someone that had to do with escapes. But we won't do that. If we want ex-Warder Cole, we know where to find him; but just now we're trying to get at this business without anyone being the wiser what we're at. So far as they know, it's only a routine raid; and if we do happen to get some fellow we're looking for on another account altogether—well, so much the better. He'll think it's someone else has shopped him, his china[1] maybe, and he'll shop him in return and we'll take whatever is sent us and be grateful for it.'

'There's Spillane's, down across Summerhill; don't waste any time now—but don't kill us either. Me nor Mick; we mightn't be as well prepared as we should be.'

Mick, the sergeant, and a third, silent detective approached the pub from the two entrances.

'Good evening all,' said the sergeant, putting his head in the doorway.

His greeting was returned in muttered curses and one man made as if to leave, though his pint was barely touched.

He bumped into the silent one at the far door, however, and was called back by the sergeant.

'Sure, what hurry is on you, Billy Boy?'

He came back to the counter. 'I suppose I can finish me scoop, anyway.'

'Of course, you can,' said the sergeant, his voice as soft as butter. 'Far be it from us to get between a decent man and his drop of nourishment. And us with a grand new automobile to take you down as far as College Street with us. Nobody else we're looking to have a bit of a chat with, I suppose? No? Well, I suppose you'd better come along with us, Billy Boy.'

The man drank up his pint and went away with them.

'Not,' said the sergeant, 'that we were looking for you at all.'

'Oh, no, not at all,' said Billy Boy sarcastically. 'I sup-

1. Pal

pose no one gave yous the bend I had an appointment here for this time.'

'Settle yourself comfortably there on the cushions,' said the sergeant. 'College Street, first stop,' he said to the driver. The car moved off. 'Billy Boy, I'd take a solemn oath——'

'That'd come easy to you,' said Billy Boy with bitterness. 'You'd never fail for the want of practice, anyway.'

'Oh, now, now,' said the sergeant, waving his forefinger reprovingly. 'I was only going to say that we were no more looking for you, that time we went into Spillane's——'

'Of course not. Yous only went in to look at the clock. Don't give me that old stuff. I know who gave yous the bend, but if he shopped me I can double-shop him. He done screwing jobs with me and without me.'

'Now, don't be jumping to hasty conclusions. The Liverpool boat was there every night for the past week, since you did that bit of a hoist down on the Point.'

'And he was fixing me for a collier to Garston, so as I wouldn't have to pass through with the passengers. But I'll fix him. I know who he met in the Shaky Man's the other night.'

'That'll wait, that'll wait. I'll dump you in here now and I'll be back round before twelve to charge you. I'm not taking you to the Bridewell, for I'm letting you go on the rent-book. I suppose she'll come down to bail you out?'

'Oh, she will, Sergeant. You know the address. But you're not codding me, Sergeant, are you?'

'I'd want to eat a few more loaves, Billy Boy, before I'd cod you; but I don't like to see people that I know is worse than the ones they lead into these things getting away with it, because they were first to the super with confessions—their own and every other body's. Even us, though we have to deal with them,' he raised his eyes piously to heaven, 'we don't like an informer. Especially a man to give away on a chap that he practically brought on a job.'

'That's it, Sergeant, that's it. Sure it was him in the first place. He——'

'That's all right, Billy Boy, you can tell me all about it, when I come down with herself and the rent-book. We're there now, hop out, avic.'

'You won't forget, Sergeant, will you?' he said eagerly in through the car window.

'Certainly and I won't and before you go in there, remember this from me. The next time you go out on a screwing job, pick a better china—go with an honest robber.'

He waved to Billy from the car. Billy waved back and was led inside.

'What was he talking about?' asked the sergeant. 'Who's his china?'

'We had him down for some snaking bit of a hoist. Cigarettes down the quay. Nothing much. They lifted them out of the back of a lorry. Just his strength,' said Mick. 'He goes to work sometimes with that fellow that they call Pig's Eye. That's why he mentioned the Shaky Man's. This Pig's Eye drinks there.'

'And he said something about Pig's Eye meeting someone there, the other night.'

'Pig's Eye wasn't down for the cigarette job the other fellow was down for.'

'Well, he's down for it now,' said the sergeant. 'I'd like to know who he was meeting in the Shaky Man's. I'll dump him in the Bridewell and neither will know the other is in. Back and forward I'll go,' his lips opening in ecstasy, 'one telling me one thing and the other telling me another.'

'And,' said the driver eagerly, 'we might pick up someone else be good luck, up in the Shaky Man's.'

'That's right,' said the sergeant graciously, 'the night's only a pup. Drive up there and we'll see.'

'Which way, Sergeant?' asked the driver.

The sergeant and Mick looked at each other and spoke

slowly together: 'A Guard that doesn't know where the Shaky Man's is. . . .'

'All right,' said the sergeant resignedly, 'you take the first on your right and the———'

The car went up the quays.

12

OUTSIDE the Shaky Man's, Glimmers Gleeson was settling himself preparatory to returning to his place of business on the bridge farther down the Liffey. He adjusted his black spectacles, settled squarely on his breast the sign: 'Blind from birth,' and reached his stick for the pavement.

An approaching car caught his attention and he looked towards it, then turned back and put his head in the doorway of the Shaky Man's and shouted hoarsely: 'Nick nick give the nick there the squad leave a drink for me there one of yous God bless you,' all in one breath. Then he turned the corner and walked quickly away from the quays.

Some of the men at the bar, Pig's Eye O'Donnell in the van, rushed out the back, through a door held open by the Shaky Man, and downstairs to a cellar. They settled themselves in the darkness and cocked their ears towards a grating above them for the sound of the squad-car. It groaned in to the kerb and they heard a door slamming, nodding to each other in the half-light.

'Go in you, Mick,' said the sergeant, 'and myself and the other man will cover the doors.'

He stood on the corner and the silent detective stood at the door in the side street.

Mick looked round the pub, nodding to the Shaky Man, who wished him a good evening. There was no one at the bar and the place was empty but for two women sitting in the snug, taking snuff from a mustard tin.

He looked in at them. 'How are you, Maggie?'

'I'm nothing the better of you,' said the older and snuffier woman.

'Not going to tell us who ran out the back, when Glimmers gave the bend we were coming up in the car?'

'If it's your time for hearing,' said the other old woman, 'it's not ours for confessing.'

He came out on the street and turned to speak to the sergeant. 'There's nobody . . .' but the sergeant was speaking to Nancy Hand and nodded to him to be silent.

'Just met this little girl coming down the street here. Going in here for a message, I suppose, Nancy?'

'I was going in for a drink, to tell you the truth, Sergeant.'

'A wonder a girl like yourself wouldn't get some better place to drink than that. And that old wing,' he rolled his little eyes in sadness, 'is enough to ruin you.'

'What can you do, Sergeant, when you haven't the price of anything better?'

'A few bottles of stout, or a drop of whiskey, even. Wouldn't it be better?' He fumbled in his pocket and took out a pound note, fondling it between finger and thumb and speaking casually.

'I suppose you didn't, be any chance, see a sign of Pig's Eye O'Donnell in your travels?'

Nancy looked at the pound note, looked up at him, and moistened her lips.

'I saw him in the shop here, a few nights ago. And do you know who was in the shop?'

The sergeant shook his head slowly.

'Eddie Collins. The fellow got weighed off in London and scarpered from Parkhurst last year. He was doing ten stretch.'

The sergeant nodded.

'You're a good girl, Nancy, and I know you wouldn't mind a man old enough to be your father standing you a

66

drink. Here's the price of one now, and take my advice lay off that old wine. Good-night.' He shook her hand, pressing a pound note into it.

She shook her head in thanks and went into the shop.

'We'll have a look in a few other places,' said the sergeant. 'Come on, back into the car.'

The car went off down the quay. The sergeant remarked to Mick, 'If we happened to run into that Eddie Collins, we'd be elected.'

'So we would be too, if we won the Sweep.' As he often remarked about the sergeant, he was all right before the films and the wireless and such came in: but now his head was full of all manner of notions of terrible cute detectives that weren't as green as they were cabbage-looking. Why wouldn't he just do his patrols in a straightforward manner and leave whatever bit of mystery there might be to cleared up by some of the new fellows that were trained up in other things besides handball and cabbage-catching up in the Depot?

'Drive down as far as Townsend Street, avic,' said the sergeant to the driver, leering to himself and chuckling behind his hand in a softly mysterious fashion.

It's a good thing, thought Mick, we haven't the television here yet or that fellow would be finished altogether.

In the cellar they heard the car move off and prepared to move back upstairs. A man at the back muttered something about Nancy Hand and her conversation with the sergeant. They looked at Pig's Eye.

'We'll leave her to Heaven,' said he.

'If she's upstairs when we go up, I'll leave her for Jervis Street,' said the man that had muttered.

'You don't say one dicky-bird to her,' said Pig's Eye, who used Edgware Road English when he wanted to say something important. 'Nor none of yous say nothing to her.'

'You're not going to let her get away with the like of that, are you?'

'Whether I am or not is nobody's business but mine and,' here he smiled, 'there's more ways of killing a cat than dragging it through a keyhole on a bit of string.'

The others chuckled, as it's called, and trooped back up the stairs.

Nancy turned towards them when they came into the bar. Pig's Eye stared at her.

'Hello, Pig's Eye, and Bowser.'

'You too,' said Pig's Eye.

'How's the form, Nan?' said Bowser.

'I'm powerful.'

'More of that to you,' said Pig's Eye, nodding to the Shaky Man. 'Give us back that gargle I left down and I leaving the room.'

'Ah, not at all,' said Nancy Hand, 'give him a fresh pint and a drop of the chat with it. And you, too, Bowser?'

'You must have met an angel,' said Pig's Eye.

'I did,' said Nancy, laughing nervously, 'a two-legged one.'

'I never heard of any other sort,' said Bowser.

'Ah, no,' said Nancy, quickly, 'it's just a few makes I had, you know.'

Bowser rose his glass.

'Good luck, Bosy,' said Nancy.

'May I never see you worse,' said Pig's Eye.

In a house on the southern outskirts of the city the Scarperer sat near a window, looking into the garden and talking to Eddie Collins. He looked from behind the curtain at a grey-clad figure walking in the garden below.

'How is he doing now?'

'Cribbing away,' said Eddie. 'He says he's no better off here than he was in the 'Joy. Except for the food and drink and smoke. Even though he drank two bottles of cham-

68

pagne today and a half-bottle of malt. Though he agreed it was the best of champagne.'

'Shows how much he knows about it. Thirty-two bob a bottle. I wouldn't rinse my false teeth in it.'

'All the same, it's an awful lot of jack, between drink and chickens, even if he does come across with the five thousand nicker.'

'Eddie avic, it's not half good enough for him.' The Scarperer gazed fondly down at the Limey, who, all unknowing, walked round in his grey prison clothes. 'My life savings, the warming of my winter's years, is he.'

'I don't see much sign of him coming across with anything except telling us all the time to let him go and to give him a proper suit and a pair of shoes, and he'd come back with the readies. My oath he would. Why doesn't he give us word where we can pick up the dough?'

'I hope he doesn't. It would embarrass me terribly.'

'The five thousand nicker?'

'He is promised to a dear friend of mine for ten times that amount. A little less, a little more, depending upon the rate of exchange. And he shall have a beautiful suit all in good time. Here it is.'

He pointed to a suit of clothes hanging in a wardrobe.

Eddie Collins looked at the label: 'Aux Trois Quartiers, Boulevard de la Madeleine, Paris 3e.'

'All the way from Paris, eh.'

'Not a terribly good one. Modest and comfortable.'

'Lugs is that fed up with him asking for clothes, he says he'd like to put a habit on him.'

'What a thing to say'—the Scarperer looked down into the garden again and looked up from his loving examination of the bald patch on the Limey's head, and smiled at Eddie Collings—'about a man worth thousands. To us.'

And he raised a glass.

13

'WE'LL go down behind the South Wall,' said the sergeant. 'You'd never know what we might pick up there.'

The driver turned on to the South Quays.

'Here,' said the sergeant, at Tara Street fire station, 'round here and straight on.'

They pulled up at a public-house on the end of the street and came in the two doors of it. Nobody moved nor took much notice of them. The publican nodded.

'Good evening,' said the sergeant. 'Not a customer do you have for us these times, at all.'

'Not since I took it over,' said the publican. 'I don't allow the sort of scruff in here that used to be here when the last man had it.'

'Bedad, no,' said an old man, wheezing in the corner. 'You could easy have caught the divil himself in it, that time. I saw him up at the counter there. As plain as what I'm looking at you.'

'He gave him three winners for the Park,' said a young docker in the corner.

'You needn't be jeering at all,' said the old man.

'Don't be minding him,' said the sergeant, signalling to the barman to give the old man a drink.

'I saw him there,' said the old man, 'and he was dressed in black and ordered us a drink.'

'Your friend for life,' said the young docker. 'Good job

it wasn't twenty year ago and he offered you a job or you'd never have overed it.'

The old man pretended to ignore him and took a sip from his fresh drink.

'Go on, so,' said the sergeant kindly.

'And the next thing we knew he had his tail——'

'Up on the counter,' said the docker, 'to pay for the drink, and said : "Take it out of that." '

The old man's indignation was lost in the laughing. The sergeant turned sternly on the docker :

'You should have more respect for an old man.'

'And he should have more for us,' said the docker. 'Encouraging cops and robbers and all sorts to come in here amongst us, having a quiet pint here after our day's graft down the quays.'

The sergeant swelled in temper, but Mick pulled on his sleeve and they joined the silent one outside and got into the car.

'I wouldn't mind,' said the sergeant, 'but that old man is a great help sometimes.'

'An agent of yours, is he?' said Mick.

'Well,' said the sergeant, wisely, 'every man should keep his agents to himself, but he has given useful information betimes.'

Like tonight, said Mick to himself : a full description of Satan, alias Lucifer, wanted for the illegal possession of a tail, last seen in Cully's licensed premises, Lombard Street South.

'Up and around by Christchurch,' said the sergeant.

They stopped at a pub near a huge barrack of a lodging house.

At the bar were a number of men. Very poor men they were by the cut of their clothes and the colour of their faces, most of them drinking cheap wine. They looked up at the detectives listlessly, but reacted hardly at all to their presence. Unlike the people in the Shaky Man's who were still practising some bit of hookery, or the dockers in Cully's who earned anything they got and were contemptuous of police and crooks alike, these were the beaten and respectable ragged ones, quiet and timid on the low diet of years.

The man behind the counter had a warm greeting for the sergeant.

They muttered fervently in country accents and gripped hands across the counter. They used the handshake known as the 'G.A.A.[1] grip',—a heartfelt coupling of strong paws—talked for a few minutes, and shook hands again before they parted.

'Countyman of my own,' said the sergeant. 'The Bull Harrigan, he comes of a great Gaelic family. One of the brothers played goalman for Garda and the other brother boxed middle-weight for the R.U.C.[2] Take a man like that to run a place like that.'

'Where next, Sergeant?' asked the driver.

'To the Floating Ballroom, up in Cabra.'

They drove out through the city, and in a big suburban public-house they found two fights in progress.

Two middle-aged men were settling a dispute about cabbage in neighbouring plots, and their wives were lending auxiliary assistance in the far part of the shop. Sitting under a large notice reading, 'No singing,' were a collection of men and women, young and old, sobbing with emotion the anthem of Greater Dublin :

> 'I've got a lovely line of coconuts,
> I've got a lovely line of bowls,
> There stands my wife, the darling of my life.
> Sing, a roll a bowl, a penny you roll a bowl.'

1 Gaelic Athletic Association
2. Royal Ulster Constabulary

'Doing a great business,' said the publican. 'Nice place, isn't it? Next summer I'm going to have a beer garden in the back.'

'Well begun is half done,' said Mick, 'already you've a bear garden in the front.'

'I suppose we can drop you off up here, Mick,' said the sergeant, 'isn't it Drumcondra you live?'

'The corner of Dorset Street will do me,' said Mick.

'I've a night's work still in front of me, with talking to this Billy Boy and looking for Pig's Eye.'

'Ah, go on, a night in the nick is not going to kill Billy Boy.'

'Well, after giving him my word,' and the sergeant laughed fatly. 'I mean this is the best time I can get him down, before he gets his night's rest over and I can bring the wife with me. Goodness knows,' and he beamed and rolled his eyes, 'what he might tell me.'

'I'd sooner me supper,' said Mick as the car pulled in to the kerb to let him out.

Pig's Eye was speaking on the telephone from a public-house in Summerhill.

'. . . and after me hearing Nancy Hand say she saw you in the Shaky Man's, I met a fellow and he said he was up in the flats and he heard them saying that Billy Boy was after being pinched but the sergeant offered to bring down his wife to bail him, and they shopped me and said about you, too, Billy Boy did, being in town, and . . . What? I'm to go somewhere, out of the way, where the people will see me. Where? Have I had a haircut lately? The barber's? Yes. I can go there. He's open till half past eight. Right, I'll do that. Everyone will see me. I'll do that.'

14

' 'NIGHT,' said Pig's Eye, seating himself on a bench.
' 'Night,' said the barber, lathering the face of the
client in the chair.

There were three others waiting and a man came in just
as Pig's Eye sat down.

'The papers are there, men,' said the barber. 'All full
box.'

'We'll know the full extent of our losses, so,' said the
newcomer, an elderly man, wearing a coat with a velvet
collar and an ingratiating smile for Pig's Eye, who he
vaguely knew as a hard chaw that ganged around the
quarter.

Pig's Eye smiled back with an effort that contorted his
left eye, used as he was to glaring out of the right.

The elderly man shuddered and bent into the paper.

'More earthquakes, I see,' he said.

Pig's Eye nodded in friendly agreement.

'All these atomic bombs,' said the barber.

'I wouldn't be a bit surprised,' said the elderly man.
'They have the world upside down.'

'You're right there,' said Pig's Eye. 'And inside out.'

'All everything is like that these times,' said the old man
eagerly, tripping over his tongue in haste to agree. 'Fellows
holding up and robbing and——' he broke off in a fear of
hurting Pig's Eye's feelings. ' 'Course, maybe the poor
devils can't do anything else.'

74

'That's a lot of malarkey,' said Pig's Eye. 'Can't they think up some stroke, like anyone else? Hard work never killed anybody.' He was thinking of his own little pool and spoke sincerely. He had heard of plots to hold him up some fine night and hoist him for his readies.

'I couldn't agree with you more,' said the old man and the barber nodded and the client in the chair shook his soapy face and everyone in the shop looked honest.

'Bowsies and touchers,' said Pig's Eye. 'The cat is what they want. That's your only man.'

'That's it, that's it,' said the old man. 'The only cure for some of them.'

'Next please,' said the barber, waving a towel at the back of the man leaving the chair.

A man at the end of the bench from Pig's Eye said: 'Well, I think,' with a grin, 'it's me.'

'So it is, too,' said Pig's Eye. 'First up is the best-dressed.'

They laughed nervously and the man slid into the chair.

'Words at will,' said the barber in a big whisper, 'hasn't he?'

In the Shaky Man's there was a concert. The Goofy One and some other ladies had emerged from the 'Joy, and one of them was singing to a respectful audience.

'Brought down the house in Huddersfield and in Maghull she had to give three encores before they'd let her in off the stage,' said a friend. 'More power, me love, I'd never doubt you. A beautiful sopranet and never lost it. Chorus now, ladies and gent's all.'

'Nancy not in tonight?' they asked the Shaky Man.

'She was here, but she went off to meet someone at eight o'clock.'

The Goofy One was crooning in the corner 'Look over your shoulder,' and 'Ould Ireland is free.'

'Shut up there a minute. The lady will favour us with an encore.'

'Encore! Give us the one you sang at the wake! Encore! Police! Encore!' they shouted in jovial humour.

The door burst open and Kilbeggan Kate nearly fell into the shop, her eyes wide and in great distress.

'What's up with the other one?'

'Hey, Kate, what's the matter with you?'

'Yous may well ask. Poor . . . poor Nancy. Opened to the world, the poor face nearly cut off her.'

'Quick, call a drink there for Kate. What happened to her?'

'Wait till she gets the drink into her.'

'Cut open,' said Kate, 'from ear . . .'

'To there,' murmured the Goofy One.

'Ah, shut up you and leave her tell us.'

'She went down the street to meet some fellow. He put it on her. Shivved her. Razor. Any thing to do tonight. No? Well,' she made the gesture of a sharp instrument drawn across the face, 'sew that up.'

'Lord between us and all harm.'

Kilbeggan Kate spoke in to the silent crowd gathered round her. 'She was carted off to Jervis Street only a quarter of an hour ago.'

In the barber's, Pig's Eye waited with the elderly man while the barber finished the haircut in the chair. He waved his towel as the man paid him and said: 'Next, please.'

'That's you, sir,' said the elderly man.

'Oh, no,' said Pig's Eye, 'we just got in together. You were here as soon as I was.'

'Oh, no,' smiled the elderly man, 'you were already sitting down when I got in the door.'

'Well maybe you're in a hurry.'

'Well, as a matter of fact, I am in a bit of a hurry. If you're sure you don't mind.'

'Not a bit,' said Pig's Eye, 'sit down there,' and with a

76

return to his more usual manner, 'don't keep this man all night.'

The elderly man sat in the barber's chair hurriedly and said, 'Certainly, and I'm very much obliged to you, sir.'

Billy Boy was followed by a man who came into the pub after him, and started an argument with him about hurling, about which Billy Boy insisted he knew nothing.

'You knew enough to insult Tipperary.'

'I don't even know where the place is,' said Billy Boy, who was anxiously looking round for support against this lunatic. But there was only the barman, keeping well to the other end of the shop.

'You don't? Well I do,' roared the man. 'Come outside and say to me what you said in there.'

Billy Boy looked towards the barman, nearly in tears.

'Out you come,' said the hurler, dragging him outside. 'Now take that and that.'

The last words Billy Boy heard before he passed out was to keep his trap shut about certain people. They had nothing to do with hurling.

His haircut finished, Pig's Eye stood up to pay the man.

'You'd a long wait, sir.'

'It's nearly quarter past nine, now, isn't it?'

'Yes, and you here from before eight.'

'That's right,' said Pig's Eye, 'and you can keep the change.'

'Oh thank you, sir,' said the barber and thought to himself that it all goes to show you can't judge the book by the cover.

15

FOR more than the fiftieth time Limey said: 'I am as much a prisoner here as ever I was in the nick.'

Eddie Collins and he were at lunch in the dining-room of an Edwardian villa on the southern outskirts of the city. There was a window behind them looking out on the garden; it was raining, had been since morning, and Limey had not been able to go out that day.

'And leaving me in these things!' said Limey, indicating his prison clothes.

'He's getting some clothes for you,' said Eddie. 'After all, you've only been taken out a few days ago.'

'He got Jerry Synnott some clothes straight away,' said the Limey.

'Jerry Synnott is not so badly wanting as you. And better than that, he has an Irish accent and can pass in a crowd. Besides, the old whistle and flute he got, you wouldn't be caught dead in.'

'Well, it looks to me like you geezers, the Scarperer and all, thought that I might take a powder and not pay you on the odds for taking me out of that drum. As if it wasn't worth five thousand nicker for me out of that lot! And as if five thousand meant that much to me.'

'We don't reckon that at all,' said Eddie. 'The Scarperer has pulled people out of the shovel and pick before now, and he never reckoned he was doing it for charity. If he didn't think you had the readies before he took you out, he'd never have started it. He's got a lot invested in this job already.'

'How is it paying him to keep me here like this? Why can't he let me go over to London, where I can get the readies and pay him and he'll be done with? I've said over and over again that you or anyone he nominates can come over with me and stay with me till I give him the gelt.'

'Listen, it's this way. We're only wanting you to stop with us till the heat blows off a little. You read the papers.' He reached for a paper from behind him. '*Police of four countries hunt escaped Englishman, search goes on for Synnott also. . . . Ports watched both sides of Irish Sea. . . . Vigilance on the Border. . . . Traffic held up in Dublin in search for escaped prisoners.*'

'Now we'll get the news.' He got up and switched on the wireless.

'. . . in the most intensive search ever carried out for escaped prisoners. The headquarters of the Garda refused to make any comments, but a spokesman for Scotland Yard declared to an agency representative that it was impossible for Watts, alias Kirke, to enter Great Britain without being apprehended. "I should regard it as equally difficult for him to leave Ireland," the spokesman added.

'The Taoiseach, it was announced today, is to travel to Foxrock on Sunday, to unveil a memorial to the men of the . . .'

Eddie switched off the radio.

'There, do you get that? It's going to be a tougher job getting you over the Irish Sea than it was getting you over the wall of the 'Joy. It can't be done just like that. You couldn't get from here to the pub on the corner without tripping over a grasshopper. And even the uniformed fellows are gone mad from thinking of the stripe they'd fall in for if they got you, or even Synnott.

'Last night they caught an old fellow going for a walk

out of his hotel. He had an English accent, because he was from London, and they pulled the whiskers off him before they found they were genuine. They sent him home with bald patches all over his face, and the commissioner's apologies for the mistake. Though, of course, they maintained it was his own fault in a way for having a beard at all and it didn't matter so much, because he was an artist or something.'

Lugs came into the room.

' 'Night, Eddie,' he said and put up his hand towards the Limey, 'and don't start off with me again about your clothes, or when you're going to be let over to England. Your starting to go there tonight.'

Limey's face lit up.

'Well, that's something! Good-oh!'

'Is he really going, Lugs?'

'Yes, I've just been talking to himself and he says we're off tonight and he wants you to go up and see him in the usual place.'

'How is it,' asked Limey, 'that I've never seen him? Even to talk to about the payment of this gelt with him?'

'He got you out of the 'Joy without you seeing him, didn't he?' said Eddie Collins, 'and he'll send one of us with you to pick up the five thousand nicker, and you'll hand it over, and that's the end of it as far as you're concerned—till you're pinched again.'

'I suppose the fees go up with each operation,' said Limey, laughing.

Eddie smiled and said earnestly: 'But you understand, none of us would last five minutes if he started coming round here. It's better that he never shows up, for himself and for all of us.'

'You better hurry right there now,' said Lugs. 'It's a fair

distance you know and he's in a hurry getting this move fixed up.'

'Yes, I suppose I'd better shift,' said Eddie. 'Good-night, all.'

' 'Night,' said Lugs.

'Good-night, old boy,' said the Limey, in quiet good humour.

Eddie Collins shut the door behind him and went into the hall.

He opened the hall door wide and shouted again, 'Good-night.'

' 'Night, 'night,' came a muffled response from the room.

He banged the hall door, stood behind it for a minute and then crept quietly up the stairs.

On the landing he opened a door and entered the front room.

The Scarperer sat in an armchair, a book on his knee, a glass of whiskey by his side and a cigar between his fingers.

'Sit down, Eddie; take the weight off your legs. Have a drink and a cigar.'

'I'll have the drink,' said Eddie, 'but if it's all equal to you, I'd sooner a Harry Wragg.'

'Every man to his taste. I started smoking cigars because they were the first kind of smoke I got my hands on. In nineteen sixteen, when I was a kid. We bashed in windows all over the place, but the big fellows got the cigarettes and we were only left with the cigars. I'd a thousand of them planted in the burnt-down vitriol works till long after Easter Week, and never smoked anything else ever since, when I had the price of them. Is your man all right, sitting up and taking nourishment?'

'Able to eat an egg,' said Eddie, smiling. 'He devoured a pound of steak and about half a cooked ham this day. I'd sooner lodge him than feed him. If he doesn't get moved out of this, it'll have been better for you to have left him up in the Old House. It's either that or he'll have us up in the Union.'

'He's starting on his journey tonight.' He put down his glass and quenched the cigar and flung it in the fireplace. 'Go down now, you, and you'll meet Jerry Synnott at the garage. You and he will drive the hearse back here and have it ready for the trip.'

'The hearse?' said Eddie.

'Yes, the hearse. Jerry has another rig-out that will do you. Top-hat, black cockade, and black top-coat. You can put your own hat and coat into the coffin and screw down the lid.'

16

IN THE sitting-room, Lugs and the Limey heard the hall
door open.

'Here they are,' said Lugs.

Eddie Collins and Jerry Synnott came in, dressed in their
hearseman's uniforms.

' 'Evening all,' said Eddie. 'Sorry for your trouble.'

'Friends of the corpse,' said Jerry.

'Bring in the box,' said Lugs, 'and we'll get on with
the body.'

The Limey looked doubtfully from one to the other.

They returned, carrying the coffin.

'What's this lot then?' asked the Limey anxiously.

'It's an idea we got,' said Eddie, 'to get past the cordon.
They're all round the city, holding up cars like you heard
on the wireless. Lugs will change into Jerry's rig-out and
Jerry will get outside the city and pick up a car where we
have it parked beyond the cordon and meet us a few miles
out of town. Then he'll dump this jalopy and we'll pick
him up and go down by car to where we're meeting the
boat.'

'And where do I start the journey?'

Lugs tapped the lid of the coffin. 'In this.'

'Now, look,' said the Limey, 'I've just about had enough
of this lark, I'm——'

'Use your loaf,' said Eddie. 'It's the only way we can
get you past all that law. They're seaching even turf lorries

and cabbage trucks. It'll only be for a few minutes.'

'A man could smother in a few minutes.'

'Not in this box, he couldn't,' said Lugs. 'Latest model, air-conditioned.' He pointed to the sides of it and the holes neatly drilled therein. 'There's people dying to get into coffins like this.' He removed the lid. 'Nice red silk lining. Cushioned bottom, every home comfort.'

'Hop in,' said Eddie to the Limey. 'It's only for a few minutes and then we get in the car.'

'I get in as I am, do I?'

'Yes,' said Eddie, 'we've clothes and everything where we're going.'

The Limey sighed and muttered a coarse expression. 'I'm sorry I ever left the nick. I just didn't know when I was well off. All right.'

He placed himself in the coffin and stretched himself full length.

'Here,' said Eddie, taking a half-bottle of whiskey from his pocket, 'that'll cheer you up till we get out of town. I suppose you could hardly use a cigarette. Mightn't do if they stopped us and saw smoke coming out of the coffin.'

The Limey took the whiskey and Lugs put the lid on and screwed it down. He gave the lid a farewell slap, turning his eyes to the ceiling and intoning sadly: 'Ashes to ashes and dust to dust: if Ellis didn't get you, well, Pierrepoint must.'

From inside the coffin sounded a kick and a muffled curse.

Mournfully he said: 'Dearly beloved brethren, let's get the show on the road.'

'Here,' said Jerry Synnott, showing Lugs the hearse-man's uniform, 'I'll give you a hand out with him and then I'll pass the rig-out into the driver's seat. You can put it on there.'

84

They struggled out with the coffin and got it into the open end of the hearse.

Jerry put in the clothes to Lugs and the hearse moved off.

They saw no signs of police activity till they reached a village on the Dublin County border.

There were cars stopped in front of them and some uniformed police standing round.

A plain-clothes man came over, reaching in his pocket for his warrant card.

'Police on duty.'

'Right, sir,' said Eddie.

'Oh, a hearse.'

'Yes, sir, Brannigan and Fahey, Malpas Street.'

'I won't delay you. I suppose you're anxious to get on.'

'We are, sir,' said Lugs. 'It's all equal to the fellow in the back.'

'You might have a bit of respect for him, or for his relatives that's paying you, if nothing else. Go on.'

He passed them through the cordon and said to his colleagues: 'Making a joke of the dead. Callous crowd that. All the one to them if it was me or you.'

'Ah, sure, I suppose a job like that would make you callous. Don't know how a man could do the like. Still, I suppose someone has to do it.'

Ten miles outside the city, Lugs spotted the car parked in a side road. 'That's it,' he said.

'I'd know that jam-jar anywhere. She has an engine like a jet plane. Fellow owns her told the tax office he keeps her for sport. Hunting, he should have said. She's been on more jobs than Springheel Jack, the Lord have mercy on him. Talking about the dear departed, we'll take your gills out of the box if you'll back up there near Jerry.'

They pulled out the coffin and the Limey got up and stretched himself.

85

'I thought I'd die in that box.'

'The better the place the better the deed: but get in the car and put a rug round yourself,' said Lugs.

'We'll drive slowly down here and go into a place we know for a drink or two and maybe a sandwich. That'll give Jerry time to get back the other yoke and then we'll go on together. OK?'

'It suits me,' said the Limey, who had recovered his good humour.

'Sit in here, in the back with Lugs, and we'll get on,' said Eddie. 'Don't be too long, Jerry.'

They went on a mile or two and Eddie parked the car in the yard of a tiny public-house.

They went in and seemed to be known, for they were shown immediately into a little room at the back. There was a slide in the wall, communicating with the bar.

Eddie spoke into it.

'Lugs, a pint of stout? For myself, I'll try a pint of stout. And you?' Limey nodded. 'And you've got crubeens. Eat a crubeen?' Limey nodded again.

The drinks were brought in with the pigs' feet steaming hot and a plate of bread and butter and salt and pepper and vinegar. And a basin of water and towels.

'The water and towel is for washing your hands when you're finished.'

'Well, try everything once,' said the Limey indulgently, stripping the foot to the toenail with a determined bite, and turning it curiously to the other side.

17

WHEN the pigs' feet were eaten and their hands washed, Eddie shoved the plates and basin through the hatch and ordered some whiskey. The conversation became general, ranging from swindles and robberies to jails and policemen. Limey also described his flat in London and went on about when he was a big man up west.

They discussed their war experiences. Lugs told of a splendid business he had exchanging cold tea for dollars with American servicemen, and Limey described his experiences as a supplier of concrete to the Air Ministry—delivering a lorry-load of the stuff, fluid, to a camp site, and taking it in one gate and out another and then back again, so that the one load was credited twice.

Eddie had little to relate. He was in the mailbag industry for most of the war, on account of a bit of salvage work in warehouses after the big fire of London, which the authorities insisted came under the general heading of looting.

Before Jerry arrived they had another whiskey and then a last one with him, to warm them up for the road.

They drove off and when they got on a good stretch of road, Eddie drove very fast. Limey complimented him on his driving and Lugs said that he himself could not drive at all.

He recalled an occasion in England when he was arrested while standing at a bus stop, and he was taken up 'under the Act,' and held on suspicion of having stolen a car and driven it along the East Lancs Road.

'That was a lie,' said Lugs, 'because I had only arrived in the 'Pool the night before. And I asked the grasshopper how many were in the car? And he said there was only one and it was me.'

'Well, that's a lie,' I said, 'and I can prove it.'

'How?' he asks.

'For the simple reason,' says I, 'that I don't know how to drive a car.'

'And how,' he says, 'can you prove that?'

'And, of course, when I thought about it I knew he was right. How could you prove you couldn't drive a car?'

'A deep question that,' said the Limey drowsily and fell asleep.

After a couple of hours Eddie stopped the car, and Jerry Synnott took over the driving-seat. Limey snored on, and Lugs muttered in his sleep, till Eddie gave him a dig in the ribs to waken him.

On a long bend, Limey woke up and read the direction plate caught in the beam of the headlights.

He sat up erect. 'Galway,' he said, 'I thought we were driving up north for a boat to the British coast. From Ulster.'

'Galway's in Ulster,' said Eddie Collins.

'It's in the south,' said Limey.

'So it is,' said Lugs, 'in South Ulster.'

The Limey grunted and fell asleep again.

They drove through a town and Eddie told Jerry to take a side road off the main road.

In the half-light before dawn Limey woke up and looked at the mountains.

'Well,' he said, 'this is like the Sahara Desert heaped up.'

'We haven't far to go now,' said Eddie. 'I'd better take over now, Jerry. I know the way from here.'

The road lay through endless rock and bog, till they turned off right and drove down to a little pier.

A fishing boat lay tied up, its engine coughing for life. They got out, and Eddie drove the car behind a cottage and followed them down to the quayside, where he spoke to one of the sailors.

'He says we're to go aboard and we'll get breakfast when he's out a bit.'

'That'll suit me,' said the Limey.

They went below and settled themselves on their coats and the rug Limey brought with him from the car.

The engine sounded more strongly, and they glided out into a narrow bay and towards the open sea.

A sailor shouted, and Eddie went up to collect the breakfast from him. There were mugs of tea, bread and butter, and huge lumps of fish.

They ate with good appetite, except Lugs, who turned green in the face as they went over the bar and into the ocean.

'Off your scoff, eh?' said Limey, sandwiching a lump of fish between two slices of bread and drinking deep from his mug. 'Not much of a sailor, if that little swell upsets you. I like a bit of fresh fish for breakfast, I do.'

'Well, you can have mine and all you want,' moaned Lugs.

'Pass it over,' said Limey, scooping the fish from Lugs' plate on to his own. 'Small donations gratefully received and large ones grabbed at. Don't you want the tea, neither? Good—oh, we'll have that, too. You can't beat the boys of the bull-dog breed.'

'You could sing that,' said Lugs faintly, 'if you had an air to it.'

'Study the decorations. It would take your mind off your sufferings.'

These consisted of a photograph of an American businessman, pinned to the bulkhead. A printed inscription on the mounting read: 'J. Ernest Bougie, 121 West Street (and corner of Astoria), Poughkeepsie, N.Y.' and all round the mounting was written in large laborious pencil: 'It is My Uncle Dan, My Uncle Dan it is, My Uncle Dan, this is My Uncle Dan, signed by Michael Conroy (Pat.), Clonaboola, Glawn, Co. Glaway, Ireland, the World.'

'Fine-looking fellow,' said Limey, 'his Uncle Dan. Another bit of bread till I rub up the last of the grease. Lovely grub.' He munched juicily.

'Heaven forgive you,' whispered Lugs, crawling up the ladder and to the side over which he hung, limp.

He came down and lay on his coat. Limey was humming a tune with a cigarette between his lips.

'You seem happy in your work,' said Eddie.

'Oh, well, you know, roaming home to Merrie England and all that. When do we see land? Some time tonight?'

'You can see it now,' said Lugs, from his bed of pain. 'The sun is just coming up.'

'How could you see it that soon? 'Course, it's only a few miles from the north coast of Ireland to Scotland. Maybe it's the Isle of Man you see. I don't think it's possible. I'll go up and take a glimpse.'

'I'll go up with you,' said Eddie. 'A bit of air would do us all good.'

They went up and could see the land in the rising sun not far off.

'Listen,' said Limey, seriously, 'where exactly are we going?'

But just at that moment, Eddie Collins seemed to get sick and leant over the rail, waving his hand. 'I'll—I'll—

explain when we get off,' and he bent to the rail again.

The Limey looked at him doubtfully and went below, when Eddie Collins straightened himself and apparently in the best of health, lit a cigarette. He went to the other side of the boat and sat there smoking till they came into a little pier and got off.

Eddie Collins spoke to a sailor and gave him some notes.

They walked up the beach and on to a narrow rocky path and towards a mountainside.

Some women passed them, carrying milk-cans and speaking rapidly amongst themselves.

The Limey stopped and looked at them. 'Look here, those women aren't speaking English. Where the blazes are we?'

One of the women noticed him looking at her and smiled and said something in greeting.

'Where are we? That's not English. You haven't brought me to England. I know what that language is. I heard a couple of them at it in the 'Joy. It's—Garlic—it's Irish!'

'Come on,' said Eddie Collins, 'and get moving before we wake the whole place up.'

18

THEY climbed a mountain, Eddie Collins, Jerry Synnott, Lugs, and Limey. Near the summit was a cottage built into the wall of a fort which made its gable end. Eddie took a key from his pocket, opened the door, and entered. He showed them the kitchen and one bedroom with three beds in it.

'Good accommodation,' said Eddie. 'Every home comfort.'

'But only three beds,' said Limey.

'Oh, well, I don't suppose,' and he looked at Lugs and Jerry, 'we'll want to sleep at the same time.'

'When are we going to get out of this drum? That's what I'd like to know,' said the Limey.

'We'll talk about that later on. I'm personally all in favour of a portion of sleep right now. It's all right for you fellows, but Jerry and I were driving all night.'

'I didn't get much rest myself,' said Limey.

'We'll get down to it so, and Lugs can see about some scoff. You'll get plenty of stuff, out there in the kitchen.'

'Right,' said Lugs, 'and it's the prayer of an old Irish skivvy that it poisons the whole lot of yous.'

'That's all right,' said Limey, 'but I'd still like to know where the hell we are and how long we're going to stop here.'

'If I knew I'd tell you,' said Lugs, washing out a pot in

the kitchen, 'but I'm only working here, the same as your-self,' and in a mock country accent, ' 'tis the master you'd want to be asking.'

The Scarperer arrived at Collinstown in a taxi, went to the Customs, was met respectfully as a practised traveller and deposited his luggage.

In the bar, he sat and smoked a cigar and ordered a whiskey for himself, till his flight was called.

His fellow passengers were mostly pilgrims, with two young men, obviously students, in great spirits and already a bit drunk.

The pilgrims were middle-aged, simple people, who had probably saved up for the trip over a long period of aus-terity. They sat, thrilled and frightened, while the engines roared and the plane taxied round the runway. They grip-ped their seats when the noises of the engines began and gazed fearfully out of the windows and shut their mouths and held their breath with some idea maybe of increasing the buoyancy of the plane. Then they saw they were still on the ground and relaxed again, till they put their faces to the window and discovered that they were already airborne, when they shut their mouths again quickly.

The students ordered drinks and one of them enquired whether this was a singing plane.

The hostess smiled the smile of the professionally polite and came down and sat near the oldest and most timid lady pilgrim and assured her that they had never yet had an acci-dent of even the smallest kind on the Dublin–Paris route.

Another pilgrim assured the old lady of the special pro-tection of Providence on account of the nature of her journey.

'I don't know,' said the old woman, sourly. 'They say the divil looks after his own and maybe it goes be contraries.'

One of the students called the attention of his friend, Séan, to the state of the wings.

In a stage whisper, he remarked on the rim of the wing which he said was about to fall off any minute.

At this, the old lady looked and anxiously watched a bit of the wing that was, in truth, shaking and trembling.

The Scarperer turned to her and in gentle tones informed her that this was a part of the plane's mechanism that was required to wobble, as she described it.

In the nasal viciousness of the North Dublin slums that seemed to come from the mouth of a different man, he addressed the students.

'Hey, fishface, because your old fellow sold enough pigs to get you as far from the bog as a university, it doesn't give you the right to go upsetting old women that aren't interfering with you!'

The students looked at him in surprise, but he looked back and they thought the better of it and muttered and ordered another drink.

He returned to his conversation with the old woman and told her what bit of sea and what countryside they were passing over as they flew on towards Paris.

She, in turn, told him she was making the pilgrimage by proxy, so to speak, for a son who was 'bad with nerves from the war.' They discovered that they knew the same parts of Dublin, though when she mentioned people that had lived there, he said he had been out of Dublin a long time.

When she asked him was he, too, making the pilgrimage, he smiled and said he wasn't, this year. He ordered a brandy, which she took under protest, because he said it was good when you were on a long journey and he was having one himself. She took one with him just to show no coolness.

They got through Le Bourget on time and sped towards

the city in the airport bus. She didn't think much of Paris at the beginning, but going round the Etoile, she gasped at the Arc de Triomphe, looked out the other side at the Champs-Elysées, and gasped again.

'Its name means "the Fields of Heaven".'

'God forgive me,' said the old woman, 'if Heaven is half as good, it'll make up for a lot.'

The old man behind her had spotted the name plate on the Avenue MacMahon.

'There was them MacMahons used to live beside us in Ballybough,' said she, 'I wonder has it anything to do with them? One of them worked on the Glasgow boat, but I never heard of his going foreign, or coming over here.'

The old man grunted and said they wouldn't be let into France. He didn't seem to think much of the MacMahons.

The travel agency man was waiting for them at the Gare des Invalides. They parted with a wish, on the old woman's side, that he drop in some evening when they were back home—giving him the address and the number of the bus and where he was to get off.

The driver looked round and the Scarperer gave him directions.

'Café Mabillon, Boulevard Saint-Germain et la rue Mabillon.'

In the Mabillon, the patron greeted him warmly, and he enquired for Madame Eugenie.

The patron smiled. 'Ah, 'Genie Etoile, oui, m'sieu.' He went round the corner and brought back with him a girl of about twenty-six, who came towards the Scarperer with outstretched arms.

They sat down and ordered a drink. He had a fine, and she said she would take an apéritif.

Over the brandy and her Cinzano with a bit of lemon floating in it, they put their heads together.

'You have news for Pierre?' said 'Genie anxiously.

'Tell him,' said the Scarperer, 'we have the article, like the description as to weight, length, width, and colour.'

'I will go immediately. It is not easy to get to him. All the flics are watching for him. Every damn agent in Paris and the banlieue. I may be away even two hours. But I will telephone you here and make the rendezvous. You have the—the—article—and——'

'I wish to arrange its delivery.'

19

THE Scarperer had lunch and sat over coffee reading the paper. In the corner he noticed an old man looking at him and smiling faintly in recognition.

'Bon jour, M'sieu le Tramtrack.'

'Ah, bon jour, M'sieu'ra.'

The Scarperer thought that all Marseillais spoke in a high tone and added a sing-song 'a' to the end of words. Other Irish people told him it was the illusion of a Cork accent, because he knew they were from the south.

M'sieu le Tramtrack was a long time in Paris, most of his life. Before the First World War, he had an accident with a tram in the Boulevard Saint-Michel, and his lawyer told him on no account to leave his bed till they were paid full damages of seventy thousand francs. The case was adjourned due to the outbreak of war and adjourned again during the Battle of the Marne and finally settled after the Armistice, though by that time the trams were gone off the streets. A new action had to be started against the directors of the tram company, which was now in liquidation, said M'sieu le Tramtrack—or, rather his lawyer, for he was still in bed hopefully studying the property market to see what little bit of land he would buy with his seventy thousand francs when he got it.

The money was finally paid over to him in full in 1946, and he got up out of bed to spend his seventy thousand francs—by this time not a matter of any great difficulty, even for a man whose sustenance consisted of pastis and hard-boiled eggs.

The Scarperer invited him to join him at the table and loudly called for his drink.

'Un Ricard, a la Marseillaise.'

'Ah,' said M'sieu le Tramtrack, 'M'sieu has not forgotten?'

Of all forms of pastis or anis, M'sieu le Tramtrack insisted that Berger or Ricard was the nearest to the original and late-lamented absinthe.

The Scarperer asked about other prominent residents of the quarter, and M'sieu le Tramtrack told him that the Veritable Sage was now in an asylum in his native New York. For long years the Sage had an Akademia of Dance and Song and Mime and Greek Living. He wore a long white beard and skirts of flannel, a leather belt, and sandals. His female disciples, half a dozen fat old ladies who came to Paris at the same time as himself, were similarly got up, except for the beard.

He returned to New York on a sort of mission, but apparently the living was too Greek for his countrymen and his message now carried no farther than the walls of the county puzzle factory.

They recalled the Feast of the Sun, when, to the music of flutes and drums, the Akademia came dancing slowly up the rue Dauphine at midnight, only to topple in a heap over a thin wire, knee-high across the narrow street, thoughtfully placed there by the students of the Beaux-Arts.

But le Mandarin was still to the good.

This was another old gentleman of uncertain nationality, but with an extensive knowledge of a branch of English Literature consisting of treaties between H. M. Government and the late Imperial Government of China. He carried copies of these documents, English text one side and Chinese the other, and was always willing to read the Chinese bit, if the English person wanted to follow it on the other page. Most of them didn't, but le Mandarin, amongst his accomplishments, had a knowledge of ju-jitsu and insisted on giving value for his entertainment.

And who was coming in the door now but the Bonapartist. He wore a long black coat and a cocked hat, which he removed and hung with his sword on the rack near the cash register. He came forward and all stood, including the Scarperer and M'sieu le Tramtrack.

'Vive l'Empereur,' they saluted him.

He acknowledged the greeting and signalled them to be seated.

'A bas les Anglais,' he said to the Scarperer, and enquired of him about Ireland, and what of her hated enemy. Was Billy Pitt still spinning his webs of intrigue from Ten Downing Street?

The Scarperer murmured that he hadn't been seen round there lately, but no doubt he was still at it as hard as ever.

'No doubt,' said the Bonapartist, and said he would have a brandy in memory of his late chief.

It was brought, and the waiter told the Scarperer that Madame 'Genie was on the phone and wished to speak to the foreigner.

'Le Lapin Agile, now,' she said and hung up.

He bade farewell to his friends, paid for the drinks and ordered another couple to be sent over, and went out.

The Bonapartist waved to him from the table.

'Vive l'Empereur, Vive de Valera, l'Empereur d'Ulsterre.'

The Scarperer bowed in acknowledgment and went down the boulevard to the Métro station at Saint-Germain-des-Prés.

He came south of Montparnasse and walked to a little street beyond Port-Royal, passing on the way the Palais du

Peuple, the Salvation Army hostel for the area, and the Santé, the big prison.

He glanced behind him and quickly went down a lane and into a café, under the wooden rabbit swinging by the ears from over the door.

The place was full of working people, poor French, Algerians, and others of various nationalities that looked as if work had never troubled them.

'Genie Etoile was sitting at a table drinking a fruit juice or looking at it.

'Ah,' she smiled in greeting, 'we'll go now.'

She went to the counter and had a whispered conversation with the proprietor, a large fat man engrossed in a dish of lambs' feet and vinegar. He nodded and said something with his mouth full, drank an enormous glass of Marsala to clear a passage for his breath, banged himself severely on the chest, and said to follow him.

He led the way, shouting for the people to hear him that he hadn't got room for the gentleman just at the moment, but he'd see what his friend across the street would do. And, of course there was also l'Armée du Salut, not so far away.

One of his customers remarked that the Santé wasn't so far away either, and M'sieu le Patron remarked, in passing, that if that gentleman had any future need of his gizzard and didn't want to be at the loss of it, it would be as well if he kept his own company.

He went across the road and into another café, called La Reine Blanche, in compliment, perhaps, to the old lady who sat behind the zinc counter, darting beady eyes from under a head of white hair and raising her massive bosom from the till as they entered.

The old woman brought them upstairs and into a sitting-room and left them.

A man sitting at the table rose and shook hands with them. He was in appearance not unlike the Limey.

'You are comfortable here, Pierre,' said the Scarperer.

'Not so comfortable that I won't be damn glad to be able to get down to Africa after I'm dead,' and he laughed. 'I saw the pictures. Just the thing. That fifty million francs is yours as soon as the matter is disposed of.'

'It's a little bit too near the Santé,' said the Scarperer, in reference to the apartment.

'Oh, that,' smiled Pierre le Fou and muttered something in unintelligible French. 'That's Corsican. An old proverb meaning, "The nearest to the wick, the farthest from the flame".'

'Just one thing,' said the Scarperer, 'the Sûreté would have your fingerprints. The poster says you did five years for wounding before the war.'

Pierre nodded to 'Genie Etoile: 'When we were children, Le Bébé Joli, someone cut his ears off.

'But they have no fingerprints. I was made a present of my prints. By myself,' he laughed, 'in February, nineteen forty-four. When I was defending law and order in Doriot's milice.'

He laughed again. 'I was a long time looking for them. No; they won't be difficult and as for the rest, after a few days in the water, who'd know the difference?'

20

'LISTEN,' said Limey, 'seeing as we're going to be bogged down in this place for some time to come, how am I going to get some exercise? Even in the nick——'

'Don't start that all over again,' said Eddie Collins wearily. 'If you liked the nick that much why didn't you stop there and not give us all this trouble?'

'Well, I'm not so sure I wouldn't have been nearly as well off. I'm first dumped in a little house somewhere beyond Dublin and then transported by land and water to some gaff that would be like the Moor only it's not so cheerful. I'm still wearing my lag livery,' pointing to his prison clothes, 'and I don't even know what country I'm in.'

'I told you before,' said Collins, 'you're in northern Scotland.'

'I always thought the Jocks spoke English like anyone else, except for a few "Och Ayes," and "It's a braw bright nicht the nicht." That wasn't what those Russian milkmaids were jabbering among themselves when we come up the camel track off that fishing boat. It sounded to me more like Garlic.'

'Gaelic.'

'Well, whatever you call it. It wasn't English. Gaelic, then.'

'Haven't you ever heard of Scotch Gaelic?'

'I've heard of Bonnie Prince Charlie. You don't think he

comes round here giving bagpipe lessons, do you? What part of Scotland are we in?'

'I've told you fifteen times, I don't know myself. None of us have ever been here before.'

'That,' says Lugs, looking out over the hill through a grey sheet of rain, 'is the truth. Nor do we ever want to be here again.'

'But you knew what direction to drive the car——'

Eddie Collins changed the subject.

'And as regards your clothes, I've told you, we hadn't a chance to get the gear yet, but as soon as you're fixed up for transport to where you want to go, that will be all arranged. As regards exercise, if you want to go out there and roll round in the wet, it's no skin off my nose.'

'We could all do with a bit of a walk or something, but it's too damn wet to stir out!'

'Let's open a nice bottle of whiskey and whisky,'[1] said Lugs, 'and we'll play poker or tell fortunes.'

'The whiskey is an idea anyway,' said the Limey.

'There's a case inside. I've seen it and I doing a bit of housework.'

'Go and fetch it then.

Lugs brought out a bottle and glasses and a jug of water.

'Take off your shawl, Maggie, there's a sup sent for.'

They had that bottle and another Scotch one. On the third round Eddie Collins and Jerry only took a half and Eddie looked warningly at Lugs as he filled his own glass.

'And that's another thing,' said the Limey, severely, 'why do you always look as if only I was to have a good bash at it? Why shouldn't Lugs have as much as he wants? It always looks as if you geezers were three screws sitting in

1. Irish and Scotch

with a condemned man and taking a drop to humour him, but not so much that you won't be able to watch him.'

'Give us all another dose, then,' said Eddie Collins, 'but you don't want to see Lugs drunk. You'd see better sights in an art gallery.'

'You're not all that of an oil painting yourself,' grumbled Lugs but for the rest of the evening, though they kept the Limey's glass well filled, they were abstemious enough themselves.

'As the Scarperer says, there's clever men and one sort of them drinks,' muttered Eddie.

'Which gives the drop to the ones who don't,' said the Limey boozily, 'but it won't work with me—The Gospel according to Saint Scarperer, whoever he is, when he's at home. I've never met him.'

'Pleasure in store,' said Lugs, 'have another. We lived through the winter and the divil wouldn't kill us in summer.'

The Limey sat looking at a pile of magazines in the sun, got tired of it, and went for a walk round the field at the back of the house.

It wasn't so much a field as an enclosed space within a circular wall. The wall was six feet thick in places and twenty feet high, except at one end, where it had tumbled down into a pile. Eddie told him that it was the remains of a fort thousands of years old. The remainder of a lagging station, more likely, because it was like the exercise yard of any prison he had known.

But it was better, Collins said, that he didn't wander outside on the hills in case the local people got suspicious of a stranger. This place was entered from the back door of the house, built into a part of its stone wall, which formed the gable end of the house. The Limey had gone back into the house for a drink, and found that they had thoughtfully locked the front door before they went out.

Scotland was north of England and if he could get out and down to a post office without running into the law on the way, it might be possible to get a telephone call or even a wire through to London, and get some money back and take a fast whip down south and away from all this lot.

That part of the wall down at the other end was low, and it sounded like a railway track in the distance behind it.

He went inside again. There were none of them back yet.

He looked around him, and—hang it, they could hardly object to him having a look round him—began the ascent. It was easier even than he had expected. The fallen stones made steps almost to the top of the wall. Up, up another bit, and the wind hit his face with a roar.

It wasn't a railway track, but hundreds of dizzy feet below, the sea in madness, beating itself to wild spray on the jagged rocks.

He trembled and reached his way down to a lower perch. Well anyway, he could go to the other side of the wall and see if the road led from there.

Carefully he worked his way from the edge and round the inside line of stones, till he was well in from it and stood on the top of the wall again.

Under him was a field but he could not see the road. But it wouldn't be difficult to clamber down the far side, if he knew what way to get on the southern road after that. He could take to the fields and work his way down alongside it.

There was an old man coming across the field with a can in his hand.

'Hey,' he shouted.

The old man saw him and came towards him, smiling over his broken teeth.

'Which way lies the southern road?'

'Yes, yes,' said the old man, smiling.

'I said, which way lies the southern road?'

'Oh, yes,' said the old man.

'——— you,' he almost shouted, 'are you deaf or what? Which way is the southern road?'

The old man understood from his gesticulations that he was asking a question and he smiled again.

'Oh, yes, ach, ni thuigimse Bearla.'

'What?'

'Ye ni thuigimse Bearla.' And he smiled again.

Lugs walked round the other side of the wall and looked up at the Limey.

Indicating the old man, he called up:

'Your gills here, he says he doesn't understand English. Ni thuigim se Bearla,' to the old man in laborious Irish, 'ta an ceart agam, da?'

'Ta'n ceart a't,' said the old man happily 'ni thuigimse Bearla.'

'And now,' said Lugs, 'before you come down off of that and break your neck, I want to tell you that lunch is served in a matter of minutes.'

The Limey gazed anxiously all round him. 'Listen,' he said, 'before you go I can see all round this drum.'

'God bless your eyesight,' said Lugs politely.

'It's an island. There's water all round it.'

'That's right. Only for that it wouldn't be an island, would it?'

21

T H E Scarperer looked at Pierre and smiled understand-
ingly.

'I think the best thing is for Armand to arrange now
with some friends of ours to go to that place. I've already
made enquiries and it seems the trawlers are going up
there all the time. Armand had made arrangements with
some people and will go with them and pick up you and the
cargo. Give them the map, and they will make the rendezvous with you.'

The Scarperer took a map from his pocket. An Ord-
nance Survey of the west coast of Ireland.

'Would it not be better if I went with them to point out
the exact spot?'

Pierre smiled, 'I've a man who knows the Irish coast
fairly well, but perhaps it is good that you go with them. It
may help him mark the map. 'Genie.'

'Yes, Pierre?'

'Both of you go and get Armand and say to him he
must go and see our friend of the fishes, and bring our
friend here along too and then they will come back here
and we will settle the business.'

'You come with me,' said 'Genie.

'And right back here,' said Pierre, 'when the business is
finished.' To the Scarperer, he said: 'Don't spend too
much time swilling that onion soup. I know what the markets are like.'

'We get the Métro as far as Gobelins,' said 'Genie Etoile.

They came up the steps and into the brightly lit streets. 'Now, along here to the chess club.'

The chess club was a long, dark café, with every table occupied by a chess-player, their noses close to the board in the bad light.

Armand was engaged in a long argument with his opponent about something, and came only when they had arranged to give the patron a card marked with the play as it stood on the board.

He shook hands with them and enquired after the Scarperer's health. The Scarperer said he was far from bad.

'You seem to take your chess very seriously.'

'Five years solitaire. It gave us an interest. We used to shout moves to each other under the cell door. That man I was playing with in the café, he was doing seven years that time, and we hadn't the game finished before I went out and had to wait two years to finish it. Where do we go from here?'

'Genie told him what Pierre had said, and he told her she could go, that he would take the Scarperer down to the markets to meet the people.

In the market they met a little man, introduced to the Scarperer as Jacques.

The Scarperer spoke politely to him in French.

The little man looked up at him, 'Don't you speak English?' he asked, and then in a flat Dublin accent: 'I'm from Raytown, Ringsend. Over here since nineteen eighteen. Married the sweetheart of the regiment. Don't tell anyone.'

'Are you the man that's going to mark the map?'

'It's marked already. I've just left the blue room and came down after yous. I'll show it to yous when we meet the skipper. And as soon as Morris Shevallyay here gives me the few balls for so doing. And then I'll shift away from yous as quick as I can. I've a chance of a porter's job in the British Hospital out in Levallois, and I'm not going round with a lot of gougers the like of yous and ruin me chances. An old one in the Legion—British, not Foreign—is speaking up for me, and I don't want to get meself a bad name. Father MacCann above in Saint-Joseph's gave me a reference too, but I don't mind him so much. He knows that Paris is full of sinners, but it'd ruin me if I was caught with a gang of bowsies the likes of yous.'

'We'll take a taxi to Saint-Germain,' said Armand.

On the way down Boulevard Raspail, the Scarperer turned to the little man : 'Would you go a pint?'

'A pint of stout? Would a duck swim? Where would the likes of me get a pint? Ninety bullets for a bottle, the size of what the women gets in the Rotunda Hospital,[1] and four hundred the draught.'

'Oh, I'll take you in and treat you,' said the Scarperer. 'I suppose we've time for the little cup, Armand?'

'Sure, the market won't be going till another hour or so.'

They stopped the taxi at Saint-Germain-des-Prés and went into the Flore.

'Janey,' said the little man, 'how do you know they'll let us in here and you not married nor a ha'porth?'

They ordered bock glasses of Guinness and the little man sunk his face lovingly into it.

'That the giving hand may never falter,' said he. 'It's years since I tasted anything but that old Beaujolais. It's worse nor a black draught, and as for the other tack, Barsac and Chablis and—I got it once the time the youngest got married—Vouvray,' he spate the great names from him, 'worse still, like what you'd give a child.'

Armand could not keep up with them, nor by the expres-

1. A Dublin women's hospital; the patients get a daily ration of Guinness

sion on his face, did he wish to, but they got through a half-dozen before they finished.

'That'll set you back a couple of thousand bullets,' said the little man, as the Scarperer peeled off notes to the waiter. 'But à bas les pauvre—put down a pig.'

They met the skipper in a little bistro behind the market and explained the map to him. The little man spoke to him in a strange language.

'Breton,' he said, 'like Irish. Anyway, I wouldn't know the difference, not knowing Irish.'

They walked back through the market and the little man gazed with disgust on the squids and crabs and strange fishes.

While Armand paid him, he spoke to an acquaintance in Italian and told him to wait a minute and he'd stand him a drink.

'Illiterate,' Armand explained, 'in seven languages.'

'Illiterate yourself, yous lot of——' he looked around '—yous lot of octopus eaters.'

He put the money in his pocket and walked away, shouting in farewell to the Scarperer. 'Thanks for the porter. Good-night and don't take any bad money.'

'Armand,' said Pierre, 'you'll go down to Dieppe to-night and bring your tattooing things. Also these,' he pointed to a suitcase. 'They might fit him better than the clothes you have. I've written a couple of letters in my handwriting that will make it appear I was—lost before I posted them. They will also serve to identify me. The money and letters you will put in this waterproof belt, which so thoughtfully I have provided.'

'What are the tattoos to be?' asked Armand. 'Travail, Famille, Patrie?'

'No, you fool. The police know I had that removed before Leclerc's Spaniards were half-way down the Avenue d'Orléans. Some of them were probably busily obliterating such things themselves. No, the last one they knew me to have was two hearts, "Mimi" in one and "Pierre" in the other, and "Mimi, l'amour éternel".'

He bowed apologetically to 'Genie Etoile. 'You must forgive me, dear, at that time I had not met you.'

'Genie Etoile smiled and nodded.

To the Scarperer he said, 'Not more than three miles from the French coast. I should like to be buried in my native waters.'

He smiled. 'And of course, if I were any farther out, I might not be found.'

22

'THIS is an island,' said the Limey. 'How long are we going to stop in this place? I thought I'd have got to England long ago.'

'I'll tell you something,' said Eddie Collins, 'there's no chance of getting into England from the Irish side just yet. You heard the one o'clock news today. They're still watching every port from Bristol up to Glasgow.'

'Can't you let me take my chance?' said the Limey. 'I'm as much a prisoner now as I'd been on the Moor. I'm not going to do you for that five thousand. One of you can come with me.'

Eddie put up his hand. 'Just a minute. I said they were watching the ports of both sides of the Irish Sea. That doesn't say they'll be watching for you at the Channel ports—Newhaven, Folkestone, Dover—or at London airport.'

'But I'm not in France. I'm in——' he looked out the window, at the driving rain on the rocks, 'Iceland or some damn place, by the looks of it. Anyway, where am I? What do you call this place?'

'That doesn't matter to you, now. We're leaving it to-night. For France.'

'For France?'

'Yes. The idea is, we take you over to France, fit you out with a French identity on the way over—clothes, papers, identity card, work-card, and even have your arm tattooed like a Frenchman. You get a boat going from the Paris docks.'

'Paris docks,' said the Limey scornfully, 'there ain't no such thing as docks in Paris.'

'Yes, there are,' said Eddie. 'The boats come up the Seine from Rouen direction and oil barges come from all over to the Quai d'Austerlitz. The boats that come from London are your interest, though. They're not big boats, but they're big enough to take you over to Tilbury—I suppose you'd know your way home from there?'

The Limey smiled and cursed fondly. 'Wouldn't I, just!'

'We'll get you on one of the boats from London, if we make it worth the bloke's while. The papers are only a bluff for them, in case they got too nosy and find out who you are. They don't speak French and you can just lie-in till you land. OK?'

'So far, so good. Anything to get out of this place.'

'You won't have to show any papers in France. We'll just take a fast whip up to Paris when we land and stop in the hotel till the boat moves off from Austerlitz. That's the name of the dock in Paris. You want the French papers, though, because those sailor blokes, if they found out who you were, might think it a good stroke to hand you over and get the reward. You're worth a couple of thousand nicker. Synnott's not even mentioned with the non-runners. Common criminal!'

Jerry smiled quietly.

'And when I land at Tilbury? Have I to show anything?'

'Certainly you don't. And make sure you've got all that French stuff, dough and all, thrown into the drink, soon as you get into dock. Just step up and chat to the people on the quayside in your Limey accent and get a bus or taxi wherever you want to go. You'll be given some English money in Paris. Now, about our end of it.'

'Yes,' said the Limey, 'we'll want to arrange about that.'

'One of us will have gone over by plane and will meet the boat where she comes in. You'll meet our man and take him up to your drum, where you can get the dough and pay him. Cash mind, no cheques,' he smiled.

The Limey smiled too, thinking what he would have done to their agent when he got on home ground. 'Oh, certainly. I'll give him the five thousand in readies and,' he smiled again, 'I'll work him something for himself and all.'

'Well, that's that. You can get dressed as soon as we get aboard. A bloke on the boat will do the tattoos and it should be here just a little after dark.'

'Do we really want the tattoos?'

'Well, they will have the idea you're on the trot from the Kate Kearney, which is the idea we want them to get; and no old soldier in the French Army ever comes out without one tattoo anyway. If you want to, you can get it removed when you get to London.'

'It won't worry me that much.'

'Well, that's that. What about a drink? As we're waiting for this fish-bateau?'

They sat drinking and smoking, looking out the window, till Lugs said that he saw a light.

Eddie went to the beach, and came back and said the men were there to row them over. Out in the bay the mast-light of the trawler swung on the water.

'Right. Lugs, stick a few bottles into a sack or something and we'll get moving.'

The boat was waiting at the edge of the beach.

One of the men muttered something in Irish to his companion and spoke to them in an American accent.

'Get in there. Squat right down on the floor, you, the fat guy.' He meant Limey.

'There's an inch of water there,' said the Limey.

'Makes no odds,' said Eddie, 'you'll be changing your clothes when we get aboard the trawler. It won't matter about your Mountjoy flannel.'

The trawler put out to sea and they went aft and had tea. Lugs got into his bunk and looked like remaining there for the rest of the trip.

They fitted the Limey with his new French clothes and gave him the papers and told him to keep them in his pocket.

He put the belt round his waist and thought so well of himself that he examined his reflection in the mirror over Lug's bunk. Eddie made a bundle of his prison rig and having weighted it, flung it overboard.

'I'm not sorry to see the last of them,' said the Limey, examining the cuffs of his new jacket.

'And that belt,' said Lugs, 'it'll be nice and handy. Save your money from getting wet.'

23

A SEAMAN stood in the doorway of the little cabin.
'I'm Armand,' he said, 'I come to put on the tattoo.'
'Oh, that's right,' said Eddie. 'Well, here's the patient,' pointing to Limey.

'We'll be a few days on this trip,' said Limey, 'why not leave it till later? I'm just settled down nice and comfortable, now.'

Armand shrugged his shoulders. 'I'm a seaman like anyone else on this boat. Your friends or mine have not chartered it. It has now finished fishing and is on its way, and if this one had not been ready we could have got another one. I'd have exchanged boats with a comrade, who for a consideration would let me be with my friends; but everyone aboard this boat does not know who you are, does not even know that there is anyone but the crew aboard. You haven't bought this boat. It's not very big, not a vapeur, but a little fishing boat. If I am not on watch or boxing fish dans le cave, I'm eating or sleeping.'

'All right, don't give us a sermon over it. I'm ready when you are,' said the Limey, sitting up and baring his wrists.

Armand sat beside him and traced in pencil on his arm a design of two hearts and inside them: 'Pierre,' 'Mimi,' and an inscription: 'Mimi, l'amour éternel.'

'Good job my wife can't read French,' said the Limey, while Armand reached inside a leatherette case for his needles and ink.

Next day, the tattoo was swelled up and puffy, but not painful. Limey seemed to take credit for this and reclined in his bunk, enjoying his food and a bottle of the whiskey which Lugs had carted from the house on the island.

A little Breton boy brought their meals and carried off the dirty plates. He was about fourteen and was constantly in a hurry, being followed all over the boat by shouts of: 'Où le mousse?' or the cook's curses when he hurried him from the galley: 'Emballagez, mousse!'

'Who's this mouse all the shouting is about?' said Lugs, having refused his third dinner. He was still sick and wished they'd let him die in peace.

The galley-boy pointed to himself and said: 'I, saire, I mousse.'

'Sha, bless you,' said Lugs, 'living on this tub, and the guts not easy in you from one week's end to another.'

The boy smiled and shook his head, not understanding, and went off, for somewhere forrard they were shouting for the mousse.

After sunset they went up on deck, and sat smoking and talking in low tones and looking out at the lights.

The mousse told them one evening as he laid out the supper that if they went up on deck, they would see the first lights of France. He seemed excited and pleased at the thought of getting home.

Eddie asked him in broken French was he anxious to get back to his petite amie. The mousse stood proudly to his five feet nothing and replied that he was: Would they like to see her picture?

He drew a photograph from his pocket and showed them a little girl of about his own age, and Eddie agreed with him she was very beautiful, and he marched off carrying his load of crockery in great satisfaction.

'Well, we're nearly there,' said the Limey, 'we'll go up and have a look at the lights when we're finished tea.'

'It might be better if we didn't,' said Eddie. 'There will probably be a lot doing on deck for a couple of hours yet because we're coming into land, and we don't want them to see us. We don't mind Armand, and the mousse is the skipper's nephew. Besides the Scarperer is coming down to see us.'

'Is he aboard?' said the Limey.

'Up with the skipper. He said he'll be down to see us tonight.'

'Well, I'd certainly like to meet him. I've heard that much about him. He goes around like the Invisible Man.'

'Not all the time,' said a voice from the door.

'Oh, hello,' said Eddie.

'Good-night to you,' said the Scarperer, going over to Lugs' bunk. 'Still sick, Lugs?'

'Bad enough,' said Lugs.

'Ah well, we'll have to do the best we can without you. How are you, Mr. Watts?' he enquired politely of the Limey.

'Very well, thank you, Mister . . . er. . . .'

'Mr. Scarperer will do, I suppose, as well as anything. I'm sorry we hadn't a chance of meeting before, but you'll understand the difficulties. I had a lot to arrange in regard to our business together.'

The Limey waved his hand. 'I understand that and I appreciate the way everything went like clockwork. Myself and the boys have arranged about the gelt when I get back to——'

'That's all right,' said the Scarperer, with a smile. 'If we hadn't thought you were a dependable proposition, well, we'd hardly have taken the trouble. But I think we can lawfully allow ourselves a little bit of relaxation now.' He drew a stone jug from his pocket. 'A drop of Calvados. Special stuff. Got it from my friend the skipper.'

He filled glasses and rose his towards the Limey.

'Good health,' said the Limey, tossing it back.

Eddie and the Scarperer looked at him, their glasses still in their hands.

'Aren't you fellows drinking?'

'As soon as I light a cigar.'

Eddie smelt his. 'I think I'll have a drop of malt first.'

He looked round for the bottle of whiskey and Limey slumped in the chair and seemed to go fast asleep.

Eddie jumped quickly to his feet and bent over him searching his clothes.

'Yes, he's got everything. Wallet, letters, and he's wearing the belt.'

They lifted the unconscious Limey up the steps and on the way he opened his eyes and moaned.

'Must have a constitution of a horse,' muttered Eddie.

'You'll be all right in a minute,' said the Scarperer, soothingly, 'as soon as we get you up to the air.'

'I—I——'

'You'll be all right in a minute. Out here, Eddie.'

The wind blew steadily in their faces when they stepped out into the darkness.

They dragged him to the rail and he opened his eyes and moaned: 'I—I——'

The Scarperer looked at him and over at Eddie, and they caught him by the seat of the pants and the collar of his coat.

He felt them lifting him and looked in a dazed and terrified appeal at the Scarperer and he struggled to scream. 'I—I—I—aaaah.'

'Now,' said the Scarperer and they heaved him over the rail and into the water and his cry was choked by the sea, and the trawler went on towards the French coast.

24

THE Scarperer and Eddie Collins came back down to the little cabin.

Lugs looked up as they poured drinks. 'Want one, Lugs?' asked the Scarperer.

'Yes,' said Lugs hoarsely, 'I could do with a sup.'

The Scarperer handed him a drink and lit a cigar.

'You'll need to be getting out of that shortly. We'll be getting in soon.'

'Yes. I'll dig myself out of it now in a minute. The sea hasn't been so bad lately.'

'No, we've got the lee of the land.'

'I suppose that's what it is.'

'Well, good luck all.'

'Good luck.'

'Good luck.'

'I suppose,' said Eddie Collins, 'we can chance another one.'

'Sure,' said the Scarperer, 'the bird never flew on the one wing.'

'We might as well be drunk as the way we are,' said Lugs, brightening up.

'That's it, Lugs, that's it.'

'Good luck.'

' 'Luck.'

' 'Luck.'

A little after midnight Armand came down with a tray of food.

'Three of you down here?'

'And Jerry,' said Lugs, 'wherever he is.'

'I've already attended to Jerry. He's been my guest, so to speak, all during the trip. The skipper nor none of the crew knew he was aboard. I'll bring him down now, when I get the chance, and when we come in the skipper will see four men go ashore. The same number that came aboard,' Armand smiled.

'He is very accommodating, is our skipper, but he would not like to think of anyone disappearing from his trawler. Seamen are so superstitious.'

They ate and drank and Lugs seemed to have recovered his appetite. As they were finishing, Armand shoved Jerry through the door.

'Get ready now,' he said, 'we're almost there.'

The Scarperer threw his cigar into a basin.

'Jerry, you wait there and give Lugs a hand out of bed after his recent illness. Eddie and I are going up on deck. Hurry up after us. The sun is coming up.'

'Come on, Lugs,' said Jerry, 'get a move on yourself.'

'OK, Jerry, I'll be with you in a minute.'

He fumbled with his clothes.

'Jerry.'

'Well?'

'Jerry,' Lugs spoke in a low, spiritless voice. 'I'm sorry.'

'Sorry about what?'

'You know what. About your gills. I heard—I heard— I heard him trying to cry out and in the water. He went in just beside this port,' he pointed his finger over the bunk. 'I heard the splash and he——'

'You'd want to keep your trap shut, Lugs; get your puss buttoned up. It's better for your health. I won't say anything, but if the others heard you—get your clothes on you and we'll get moving.'

They went ashore in the half-light of morning and piled into a car with Armand. It was a big Delage and once on the main route, ate up the distance.

They reached Paris by lunch-time and Armand took them to a hotel on the Left Bank off the rue du Bac.

They ate in a restaurant in the quarter and the Scarperer told Lugs that Wolfe Tone had lived in the street and might well have used the same restaurant.

'Is that so?' said Lugs. 'He was from Stafford Street, wasn't he? You find them everywhere. Fellow in the next cell to me in Brixton was from Ash Street.'

'As soon as I get you fixed up with your cut you can go home, Lugs. I don't think you want to spend too much time here.'

'Well, no. If it was a kind of trip that you weren't on business like and could tell the boys at home you were over here, I could make up a few lies about the Follybejare and that would be different. But when I can't be telling about it, it's a dead loss to me. I mean most people only come here to tell people at home about it, isn't that all?'

'That's about the height of it. Still, you might as well enjoy it while you're here. How about some champagne?'

'All right by me.'

Lugs filled and refilled his glass and waved a pile of notes which the Scarperer had given him, as a kind of advance. He called the waiter.

'Hey, garsain, gorsoon.'

For the first time since they left Ireland he was in good humour and even called on himself to sing a song about his native land. He had a good strong baritone, and rich in liquor, it carried round the room.

'Oh, the winds that blow across the Kimmage Quarry,
Are perfumed by the leather as they blow.
And the old ones in the tip-head picking cinders
Speak a language that the clergy do not know . . .'

The Scarperer waved his cigar in time to the tune.

Armand made an arrangement with the Scarperer to see him later, shook hands all round with an extra handshake for Lugs, and left them to it.

The patron knew Armand and stood listening to them, a civilly indulgent smile on his face.

They paid their bill and left and went up as far as the Mabillon, for a café fine. The Bonapartist was there and joined them in a drink and kissed Lugs on both cheeks, Lugs being under the impression that he was meeting Napoleon himself.

They parted from the Bonapartist, and the Scarperer suggested they go across Saint-Sulpice, up the rue Servandoni, over the Luxembourg, and into the Boule-Miche and have one there.

Eddie Collins remarked to Jerry Synnott that he had never seen the Scarperer in such form. He was as carefree as a boy on a school treat.

They got in on the path to let an elderly woman pass. She went on to the corner of the rue de Vaugirard and looked down at them as they approached, and then turned her attention to the biggest poster on a street hoarding.

High up on the wall it showed a photograph of a clergywoman, or a lady with a huge, pearly smile, orange lips and platinum hair.

The text was in English and read: 'American Cultural Centre of the Left Bank. Direct to Paris from West Chuzzlewit, Mass. The Rev. Mrs. Moore will deliver her famous lecture: WHAT MAKES THINGS HAPPEN.'

They looked at this with some interest and Lugs began

to serenade the picture with, 'Don't have any more, Mrs. Moore.' They went towards the gardens across the road, arm in arm.

The elderly woman ran in front of them and shook her hands in their faces and in a Monkstown accent, that sounded like South Kerry on the alien air, screamed with fury:

'Murderers! I followed you from Dieppe, though it cost me dear in the car. Murderers! Murderers!'

Lugs looked at her in amazement and in horror as he realised what she was screaming.

'Murderers!'

He roared in terrified fury. 'Shut up, shut up, you old——'

The others tried to restrain him, but he went forward and shook his fist in her face.

'M U R D E R E R S !' she screamed.

'That,' said Lugs and struck her in the mouth.

The others caught him by the arm and rushed him through the park.

The elderly woman rose and muttered through her bleedings lips: 'Murderers, murderers of our dumb brother!'

25

THEY went through the Luxembourg Gardens, Eddie and Jerry Synnott holding on to Lug's arms.

He trembled in every muscle and muttered: 'Her brother, her brother.'

They went into a café on the Boulevard Saint-Michel and took a table at the back. Lugs muttered and trembled and looked grey in the face. Jerry and Eddie were thinking hard about the old woman and even the Scarperer was puzzled and shocked.

'Stingers, I think, all round is the act,' said the Scarperer.

He called over the waiter and gave the order: a glass of cognac and a measure of crême de menthe each.

Lugs drank his right off and indicated to the waiter by signs that he wanted another round.

'Calling us murderers and in the public street!' said Lugs. 'Good job the people didn't understand English, or she'd have made a show of us.'

The others laughed, but Lugs was very serious; he seemed to be unaware of them and to talk from his own bewilderment alone.

'Murderers,' he muttered, 'murderers.'

'Oh, give over your muttering,' said Eddie Collins wearily, 'or you'll have us moidered from it. Forget about it, get it out of your head.'

'Who was she?' said Lugs.

'We don't know who she was, nor anything about her. I don't think she knows anything about us either. She was some old madwoman. Paris is full of them.'

'She was Irish.'

'Well, mad old Irishwoman. There was never any desperate shortage of them, either.'

'Murderers—how well she knew that!'

The Scarperer turned quickly in his chair and shoved his eyes hard into Lugs. And his face very close asked quietly, 'How well she knew—what?'

Lugs shook his head and seemed to waken from his daze. 'I—I—only meant—that——' he gulped and lowered his eyes from the level of the Scarperer's. 'I only meant——' he could not finish the sentence.

'You only meant that you had a dream and you were on a boat and you had your ear to the porthole and you heard a splash and someone struggling in the water and you came to Paris.'

Lugs' face was white and his jaws worked feverishly. He tried to rise from the table, but the Scarperer gripped him tightly by the wrist, so that he leant over it.

'And an old woman came up to you in the street and called you a murderer.'

Lugs broke from him and staggered to the toilet door and shut it behind him. There were sounds of someone being violently sick.

'It's equal to me,' said the Scarperer, very earnestly and in his native North Dublin tones. 'As soon as I collect for this little stunt and pay you fellows, you can go where you like. It's all one to me. I'll be far from Dublin or Paris either. But if you aim to hang round Ireland or England, it'd be as well for the good of your health if that Lugs kept his puss tight. I'm giving up work and going to live on me money a long way from the Five Lamps—new papers, new name, new nationality, new me, as a matter of fact.

But you want to keep a tight eye to that Lugs and see he doesn't go grasshoppering round the place.'

Lugs came back, wiping his face with a handkerchief.

'Feel better, dear?' said the Scarperer, in a mock-falsetto, and in his ordinary voice: 'Sit down, mouth almighty.'

Lugs sat.

'Like a drink, Lugs?'

Lugs shook his head. 'Don't feel like it.'

'Ah, we'll fix you up in a minute. Garçon!'

The waiter brought a bottle of black liquid and the Scarperer told Lugs of the great healing powers claimed for it.

'You can read all about it there on the label.'

'I can't then, because it's all foreign.'

'Oh, you'll find it in English there, too.'

Lugs read a long announcement in small type closely printed and swallowed his drink, without taking his eyes from the label till the waiter removed the bottle.

'Begob, it cures you all right,' said Lugs.

'Do you feel the better of it?' asked the Scarperer. Lugs nodded.

'Shows you the power of faith. I've been trying to cure myself on and off with that stuff for years and it never did me any good.'

'We'll have a few here and after that we'll go to a show. I'm not seeing our friends till tomorrow night, and if you see a few young women for a change, Lugs, it'll take your mind off the old ones.'

Though, as he remarked afterwards to Eddie Collins, it still didn't answer the question: Who was she?

In the pension on the corner of the rue Lhomond and the rue des Irlandais (that's what they call it) the elderly woman sat in the room having her face bathed before being put to bed by a girl of about twenty-three.

'You'll have to rest first, Aunt Jeannie, and then we'll go

to the police together, and if they don't help us, to the Embassy. But you must rest first. A couple of hours' sleep and you'll be a different woman. And I mustn't let you out alone again. Those men would stop at nothing.'

'No, the brutes. But the organisation trusts me to track them down and to put an end to their savagery.' She sat up in the bed. 'It's murder, Nancy, and——'

'I know, dear; but just rest yourself a little and then we'll both go out and attend to this business.'

'Worse than murder,' said Aunt Jeannie, settling herself on the pillows, 'if you knew what went on on that boat.'

26

AUNT JEANNIE and Nancy went early next morning to the station in Saint-Sulpice. A bored Brigadier de la Paix took a statement from her and promised to do all in his power to track down her assailants. She sniffed her way out of the station and said she hoped so, that she was on her way to her embassy and the representatives of her country would expect to hear within a day or two what steps had been taken.

The sergeant, for the benefit of his colleague, tapped the side of his head as they went out.

'Middle-aged Englishwoman——'

'Irish,' said the other policeman.

The sergeant shrugged his shoulders. 'Same thing; only themselves can tell the difference. In Paris, she expects adventures, admits herself she spoke to these men first, accosted them on the street, abused them.'

'I wouldn't mind rushing to the defence of the younger one,' said the policeman.

'No,' agreed the sergeant, 'that would be a character from an entirely different opera.'

'She threatens us with her embassy.'

The sergeant laughed. 'Yes, maybe they'll send a warship up the Seine to shell the Hôtel de Ville, if we do not quickly capture her assailants!'

'I'd sooner face their sailors than their soccer players,'

said the policeman, in whom memories of an International at Dalymount rankled.

'Ah, les étrangères,' sighed the sergeant. He placed Aunt Jeannie's report on a pile of documents dealing with the trials and troubles of foreigners in his district. An American gentleman complained that an Arab had charged him very dearly for admission to a film show entitled *Les Exotica,* which, to his disgust, consisted of lantern slides dealing with the plant-life of Indo-China. There was also a complaint from an Iberian anarchist who had been assaulted by a White Russian and an anti-Tito Yugoslavian. A travelling Turkish naturalist on his way to the United States on a mission scholarship, had lost his pocket Bible and two hundred dollars while he and a brother naturalist were talking to two ladies outside the Châtelet music-hall.

The American he got rid of by telling him to be more careful with his exotica in future and he went off muttering: 'Three thousand francs to see a flower show and they weren't even moving.'

The Turkish naturalist's misfortune had befallen him across the river and out of the police district, but there still remained the case of the Iberian anarchist.

Wearily the sergeant took up his pen and wrote:
'Miguel Cervantes Gallaborda, Passeport Nansen, Numéro. . . .'

Aunt Jeannie and Nancy travelled by Métro to the Irish Embassy. This was in the rue Paul-Valéry, off the Avenue Victor-Hugo, so they changed at Châtelet and got on the line for the Etoile, which runs under the Champs-Elysées and finishes at the Arc de Triomphe.

They came up into the sunny afternoon and Aunt Jeannie looked about her as they prepared to go round the Etoile.

'Dear me,' she sighed, 'I can't think why it is Paris recalls to me the days of my childhood.'

'You weren't at school here?' said Nancy.

'Certainly not. I was at Alexandra.[1] My dear father thought French finishing schools were half-way to Rome in more ways than one. But yet I get a distinct, sweetly melancholy, remembrance of things past. The statues, the trees, and the Bois do so remind me of . . . I. . . .'

'Phoenix Park in the days of good King Edward and the Lord Lieutenant's carriage and outriders going past the Gough Monument at a spanking pace. Pappa raises his grey bowler and Mamma tells little Emily to wave and Nancy lifts the baby from the perambulator, to see the nice mans and ladies and the lovely horsies. The lower orders rush from the playing fields of the Fifteen Acres to remove their caps and shout lustily, but with devotion : "Long life to your honour." And the dignified figure in the carriage leans foward and graciously bows as the carriage bowls along.'

'But that's exactly it, Nancy, how ever could you have known? Your poor mother was only a baby then. You seem to remember it almost better than I.'

'I sit beside two Americans at the Foyer des Etudians. They're doing a thesis on James Joyce. By the way, Aunt Jeannie, you wouldn't happen to know the price of pigs' cheeks in June, nineteen four, would you?'

'Certainly not. Look out there, Nancy.' The taxi missed them.

They reached the top of the Avenue Victor-Hugo and went down the right-hand side, looking for the rue Paul-Valéry.

'Victor Hugo. He lived as a boy in a house off the rue Saint-Jacques. Rue des Feuillantines. I knew a fellow from Dublin had a room in a hotel there and went back to Dublin without paying his rent.'

1. A Dublin girls' school; Protestant

'Indeed. I think this is the street.'

They arrived at No. 37 and Aunt Jeannie looked up at the tri-coloured shield over the gate.

A Frenchman opened the side door and looked at them.

'I wish to see my ambassador,' said Aunt Jeannie.

The Frenchman looked her up and down.

'I said that I wished to see my ambassador.' More menacingly this time as if there were every reason to believe that the Frenchman had her ambassador hidden in his pocket and was keeping him there for some low, Latin purpose of his own.

At last the Frenchman brought them across the courtyard and directed them to a waiting-room, where they were joined in a few minutes by a young man, wearing a dark suit, spectacles, and a Fianne.[1]

He brought them up to his office, gave them a cigarette each, and sat with them while Aunt Jeannie told her story.

'I see your mouth is still bruised,' he murmured, sympathetically.

She waved her hand. 'That's nothing. I knew I was taking a risk when I consented to come here for the organisation.'

'Might I be told the name of your organisation.'

'Certainly. The Irish section of the International Society for the Defence of the Horse.'

1. Gold lapel pin that indicates wearer has passed examinations in and speaks Gaelic.

27

'I SEE,' said the embassy fourth secretary, 'you came from Ireland on behalf of the Irish——'

'Section of the International Society for the Defence of the Horse. I arrived at Dieppe the same time as the ship that brought the horses and made enquiries as to where they went when they left the port. But I could get no information, and I would not have known anything more but for the fact that my hotel was on the outskirts of the town. In the early morning I heard through my open window some men speaking English and saying they were going up to Paris.

'They had Irish accents, and who else could they be if they were not concerned in this business? What would Irishmen be doing in a French port at six in the morning?'

'What else, indeed?'

'I knew they were on their way to the slaughterhouse, which is in the rue Vaugirard. I got out of bed quickly and dressed myself and hired a car, at great expense, and caught up with them in Paris, where I lost them. But for some time I remained in the Vaugirard district and at last my patience was rewarded.'

'You received a blow in the mouth,' murmured the secretary, compassionately.

'Yes, I waited till they came to the corner, hoping to follow them to the slaughterhouse, but they must have become suspicious because instead of going right, and up the rue Vaugirard, they went straight across the road and across towards the Luxembourg Gardens. And then—and then— I am afraid my feelings got the better of me and I—I— called them names. "Murderers," I shouted, and so I consider them, if you knew the sufferings of their poor victims on the ships!'

'Of course they might say that they were on their lawful business,' said the secretary. 'After all, cattle dealers are not shouted at in the streets of Dublin. On the contrary, except for publicans, there is no body of men so highly respected in our dear country from Drimoleague to Sandy Row——'

'I see we are wasting our time here, Aunt Jeannie,' said Nancy. 'The official view would appear to be that these ruffians had a perfect right to beat you.' She rose from her seat.

'No, no,' protested the secretary. 'I certainly do not think that they had any right whatsoever to treat your aunt in such a fashion. Pray, sit down a moment.'

Nancy resumed her seat.

'I only wish to point out to you the difficulty of interesting the police in such a matter. So far as they are concerned, these men are engaged in legitimate trade with this country and they might regard it as being a little unwise of a person to interfere with them in the prosecution of their business. They might even think the assaulted person was at fault in speaking to them first, when they had not given her any reason to do so, or to suppose that they wished to converse with her, or have any discussion with her about any subject whatsoever.'

'That,' said Nancy, 'is the Civil Servant viewpoint in the language of diplomacy.'

The fourth secretary inclined his head. 'So I do not think, that we, as an embassy, could do very much in the matter. But all the same . . . if you could identify these men and if I could know their names or what they look like, there are numerous ways in which they could be taught that punching ladies in the mouth is not an argument for or against the export of horses from Ireland.'

Nancy reached across the desk and shook his hand. 'Bravo, Mr.——?'

'O'Donnell is the name. You may call me Hugh.'

'And you may call me Nancy, Red Hugh O'Donnell, the northern chief.'

'Dear me,' said Aunt Jeannie, 'I always thought he was a Liverpool Communist.'

'Well, this Hugh O'Donnell, although not a chief, is from Donegal and very much at your service. I'm finished here in the office just now and I can run you down to your hotel. It's in the Latin Quarter?'

'Yes. Aunt Jeannie is staying with me in the rue Lhomond, near the Collège des Irlandais.'

'Perhaps we might see something of our friends on the way. You saw them in that district before.'

'Well, if it's not too much trouble,' said Aunt Jeannie, 'I should be very grateful. I certainly do not relish the prospect of the battle of the Métro, just at this time of the evening.'

They drove to the Boulevard Saint-Germain and Hugh O'Donnell offered them a drink.

They sat outside the Deux Magots, and Hugh called the waiter.

Nancy took a Dubonnet, and Hugh ordered a beer for himself.

Aunt Jeannie cleared her throat and looked on the table. 'Do you think, Mr. O'Donnell, that I might have a drop of Irish whiskey?'

'Dear Aunt Jeannie,' said Nancy, 'how wonderful!'

'I feel the need for a little stimulant,' said Aunt Jeannie, rather stiffly.

'Oh, I was only thinking that André Gide, in his *Journal,* also speaks of drinking Irish whiskey in Paris.'

'Well, merely because I have had rather an exhausting day and feel the need of a little pick-me-up, I can hardly be compared to a—a—journalist, in the matter of drink.'

'Not at all,' said Hugh, beckoning the waiter again as Aunt Jeannie downed her whiskey with a practised hand.

'Bon jour, 'excellence l'Ambassadeur.'

A tall figure in early nineteenth-century dress leaned across the terracing.

Hugh looked round in some dismay. 'The Bonapartist,' he muttered.

The Bonapartist saluted the ladies, gravely.

'Irish, too?'

Hugh nodded.

'Many Irish people in Paris, just now. Yesterday I spoke to three of them.'

Hugh looked at him intently. 'Where?'

'On the Boulevard. In the Mabillon.'

'Could you describe them?'

The Bonapartist could and did.

Nancy was excited. 'It's—it's——'

Hugh nodded. 'I told you there was every chance of getting a lead, as they call it.' He turned to the Bonapartist. 'You haven't seen them today?'

'No, but I think it likely they will be in that café again. I could watch.'

'If they come in before six in the evening, ring this number, Passy 1923,' Hugh wrote on a piece of paper, 'and if after six, this one, Anjou 4186.'

'And I shall say nothing? I understand.'

'And,' Hugh reached in his wallet for a thousand franc

note, 'in case you haven't change for the *jeton* of the telephone.'

The Bonapartist gracefully pocketed the money.

'Vive l'Empereur,' said Hugh.

'Vive l'Irlande. Chang Fung.'

'Chinese,' said Aunt Jeannie. 'Remarkable man, I must remember that. Chinese for farewell, "Chang Fung." '

'I think,' said Hugh, 'he was trying to say "Sinn Fein." '

28

IN HIS apartment off the rue des Cordelières, Pierre was reading the morning newspapers with great enjoyment. The old woman who brought him his coffee and croissant was a simple old soul from the townland of Rambouillet, in the middle of the plain that lies between Paris and Chartres, where the President of the Republic has his summer residence and on the Versailles road. There must have been something in that grim district, something in its flat monotony that appealed to the great, for no ordinary mortal, Royalist or Republican, would take a present of it. Madame Mimette agreed with the kings and presidents and thought it the most wonderful place on earth.

Pierre laughed and clapped his hands as he read the papers.

'M'sieu has won something in the lottery?'

'Well, it's not that.' To change the subject: 'Does Madame wish to read the winning numbers?'

Madame smiled, the inscrutable smile of a thousand years of practice with sheep.

'No, no, m'sieu. I gambled once in the lottery, but neither lost nor won.'

'Someone made Madame the present of a ticket?'

'No, m'sieu, I bought a tenth myself. And though I didn't win, my last three numbers were in a result, so I had another chance. But I was prudent and sold it to a neighbour for what I'd paid for it.'

'And it won a prize ten thousand times more valuable?'

Madame Mimette shook her mutton-head shrewdly and smiled again, the smile that boiled a thousand cabbage pots.

'No, m'sieu, it lost.'

And silently she gathered up her ware and went from the room.

'Maybe it's as well that old woman is half potty,' said Pierre to himself, taking up the late morning *Combat.*

At twelve o'clock, 'Genie and the Scarperer came to see him.

'You sent for me early this morning, Pierre,' said the Scarperer. 'Beautiful young women———'

'Genie smiled.

'———calling to my hotel early in the morning. The concierge will be getting ideas.'

'Your reputation is quite safe if your correct nationality is on the affiche. Irishmen are made for drink but afraid of women.'

The Scarperer nodded politely.

'But I could kiss every Irishman and woman this morning that was ever born! If I were not a Corsican, I should be an Irishman.'

'That's more than civil of you.'

'You have not seen this morning's papers?'

'No, I seldom see any French paper these times except *Samedi Soir.*'

'Listen to this.' Pierre took up the papers and began reading the headlines:

'PIERRE LE FOU DÉCOUVERT NOYÉ
'CADAVRE RETROUVÉ ENVIRON DE DIEPPE.

'The body of the much wanted gangster was taken from the sea near Dieppe early this morning. The body was iden-

139

tified by general physical characteristics and by a tattoo on the left wrist and by papers and letters in the dead man's handwriting discovered in a belt which the late Pierre was wearing when he went into the sea. No marks of violence were found on the body, and it is thought the gangster was alive when he entered the water. Foul play is not suspected, and the police incline towards the theory of suicide, due to the extreme strain of the hunt, which was nationwide and at times extended to Italy and Switzerland.

'My dear, dear friend,' he turned to the Scarperer, 'I congratulate you, and from the bottom of my heart I thank you. . . .'

' 'Genie, my own one!'

They embraced and she murmured, with a sob, 'My lovely drowned corpse.'

'My own sweet widow.'

Pierre straightened himself and recovered his composure.

'Tonight, I invite you all to dinner.' He looked at the Scarperer. 'You will tell the boys. It is as much their celebration as ours. We dine at eight o'clock. And it will be a meal to remember.'

'Here?' The Scarperer thought La Reine Blanche's talents were in the line of calves' feet in vinegar. They were all right, he supposed, if you could get used to the fur.

'No. That old woman would poison you. Down the Quarter.'

'But, Pierre,' said 'Genie. 'I——'

'I know, I know, you're going to tell me that it's dangerous. I'll be seen on the grands boulevards. I've no intention of being seen anywhere, till we get down to North Africa in a few days' time. We'll drive down to the Quarter, and in the rue Saint-André-des-Arts there is a little soup-shop called the Bouillon. There will be nobody there to trouble us, and the food is whatever you care to pay for it. That's not going to trouble us!

'Besides, dear,' he smiled at 'Genie, 'your own little Pierre is dead. Found drowned.'

'That's a date, so,' said the Scarperer. 'I'll wait with the boys in the Mabillon, and 'Genie can give me a ring on the phone and tell us when it's time to come round. I know the street. It runs from Place Saint-Michel into the rue Dauphine.'

'That's right,' said Pierre, 'you come down the rue de Buci, and it's just opposite you. 'Genie will give you full directions tonight.'

'I'll be off so, now,' he gave each of them a shake of the hand. 'I'm sure you two have a lot to say to each other.'

They were already saying it.

'My own pigeon-pie.'

'My cactus.'

The Bonapartist was at his stand when they came into the Mabillon, and the Scarperer called a drink for him.

He saluted the memory of the Emperor and toasted their various native lands and when the Scarperer had come back from a visit to the telephone booth, he asked, 'And your two friends, too, m'sieu. They also are Irishmen?'

The Scarperer said they were.

'Oh, m'sieu, you don't know how happy it makes me to know that.'

The Scarperer translated this, and Lugs said the old geezer must be terribly easy pleased and they must leave him a drink before they left.

Which they did. Not that he was long after them. He finished his drink in a gulp and walked a number of yards behind them and well into the shade, till they reached the Bouillon in the rue Saint-André-des-Arts.

Then he went back to the Mabillon and made a telephone call himself.

Mr. Hugh O'Donnell answered him on the phone and said he was to remain in the café till Mr. O'Donnell and two ladies came down. He was on no account to leave, and anything he wanted in the line of drink would be paid for when Mr. O'Donnell and the ladies reached the Mabillon.

The Bonapartist ordered a bottle of very old brandy and sat waiting.

29

DURING the meal, 'Genie Etoile told Pierre for more than the second time that she thought it unwise to come so far down the city, when they could have eaten up in La Reine Blanche.

'Listen, loved one,' Pierre reassured her, 'don't you believe what you see in the papers? All of them, from *Figaro* to *Humanité,* whatever else they disagree upon, are sure of one thing, that Pierre le Fou is dead. That his drowned body was taken out of the sea near Dieppe nearly twenty-four hours ago.'

After a couple of brandies she cheered up and rose her glass with the rest, to the toast: 'Pierre est mort. Vive Pierre.'

Lugs was in singing form.

'The people living out in Ballyfermot.
If they miss the last bus home, they're all at sea.
They get out their map and compass, and face westward.
To begin the long march home from Aston Quay.'

In the succeeding verse he substituted 'Saint-Germain-des-Prés,' and 'Genie, who understood nothing else, shouted: 'Bravo.'

The Scarperer laughed and waved his glass at him. 'You're coming on, Lugs. French in three days.'

The Bonapartist had made good progress with his bottle of brandy when Hugh O'Donnell and Aunt Jeannie and Nancy reached the Mabillon.

He put his fingers to his lips in conspiratorial fashion when they entered, carefully replaced the cork and returned it to the patron for future reference, while Hugh paid for it. He motioned them slowly out of the café and down the street. They followed a few yards behind him.

Aunt Jeannie walked on the inside and for further security, Nancy asked Hugh to remove the Fianne from his lapel, in case their violent countrymen came on them unawares.

'In Paris it's a sure means of getting directions if you don't speak French,' whispered Nancy. 'A black man or a person wearing a Fianne will always be able to direct you in English.'

The Bonapartist stopped at the Bouillon.

'This must be the place. I hope they're still here,' said Hugh.

There was light and noise coming from the back of the little restaurant, but the handle was out of the door and the curtains were drawn.

'It looks like a private party,' said Nancy. 'We must plan our next move.'

'And now for the dessert,' said Pierre.

'We've had it,' said Eddie Collins.

'You've had baba au rhum, and I've had an ice. But I'm talking about something better than that. Nice things for my guests.' He smiled benevolently and reached under the table and brought up a small suitcase which he placed on the table and opened.

'Ooohs' and 'Ahs' of child-like admiration went round the table and well they might. The case was packed with wads and layers of thousand, five-thousand, and ten-thousand franc notes, all new and clean.

Even Jerry Synnott sighed with enjoyment at the sight of so much money. And Lugs' rough old face shone with happiness and would have been a pleasure to look upon, if they hadn't all been so busy looking at the money.

'There will be some for everyone,' said Pierre in a kindly voice.

'Like Alfie Byrne's parties,' said Lugs to Jerry Synnott, 'when we were kids at school. Only,' he added hurriedly, 'better, much better. For when all is said and done, you can't beat the readies. I don't care what anyone says about it.'

'I think it would be best for Aunt Jeannie to have a look in at them and be certain they are the right people before we call a policeman,' said Nancy.

'All fine and large,' said Hugh, 'but the question is, how are we going to get her in? That place seems very definitely booked out for the evening. Admission by invitation only.'

'If our friend here went to the window and rapped and told the proprietor some story about my wanting a room——'

'I don't think it's a hotel.'

'They can tell us that when they've opened the door. By that time, Aunt Jeannie will have had a look over my shoulder and identified them.'

'That's if the Bonapartist will do it.'

He would, though his reluctance to be further involved with the business had to be overcome by promises of vast rewards. The people of the Bouillon were not the sort of people he wanted to be tangled with.

He rapped on the window, and after a while a woman came, drew over a corner of the curtain, and looked out. She waved to him to go away, but he persisted and at last she opened the door and asked him what the devil he wanted.

Nancy came out of the darkness and in her best French, began some story about looking for a nice room in the Quarter, and Aunt Jeannie leaned over her shoulder and looked up at the lighted end of the room and the people sitting round the table.

The woman said crossly that there were no rooms there and that old fool of a Bonapartist could direct them to a hotel and banged over the door.

'A man and a woman had their backs turned to me. But the one who struck me sat facing us,' said Aunt Jeannie. 'I've no doubt about it!'

'You remember him?' asked Hugh.

Aunt Jeannie rubbed her mouth. 'Am I ever likely to forget him?'

'Wait here, Nancy, with the Bonapartist. He——' Hugh looked round. 'He seems to have disappeared.'

'I'll wait anyway. I can make myself less noticeable in the hallway of that hotel across the road and still have a good view of the door here.'

'Good girl. Aunt Jeannie and I will go round to the police station and get them to send round a couple of agents. A couple of months and a heavy fine may put beating women out of their heads for some time.'

At first, the police were not anxious to trouble themselves with this row between foreigners, but Hugh showed them his diplomatic passport, and they said it would be no harm to send round a couple of men to have a chat with this woman-slapper.

'Deschamps, you and Monti go round with this gentleman and see this person.'

Hugh, Aunt Jeannie, and the policemen walked out of the station and round the corner, towards the restaurant.

Pierre paid the Scarperer in full and in cash. Five hundred bundles of notes. Ten ten-thousand franc notes in each and an elastic band round them.

'You'll want this, now,' said Pierre, giving him the suit-case. 'I'll split the rest with the boys.'

'Oh, no,' protested the Scarperer, 'that's my expense.'

Pierre waved his hand. 'You make your own arrange-ments with your employees. This is a little pourboire, shall we say?'

He counted out the notes and Eddie Collins and Lugs and Jerry Synnott stuffed their pockets with them.

The Scarperer raised his glass.

'Pierre est mort. Vive——'

The door burst open, and 'Genie turned and saw them first and screamed: 'Pierre, les flics,' hysterically. 'Oh, Pierre-ot, les flics.'

The two agents ran into the room. Hugh and Aunt Jeannie and Nancy behind.

Pierre turned, drew an automatic from his pocket, screamed at the Scarperer unprintable, vile abuse, and fired at him, again and again. The Scarperer slumped in his chair, his eyes filled with horror and amazement and his mouth twisted in the agony of sudden death.

'The Judas comes with me!' shouted Pierre.

There wasn't much between them, because a bullet hit him in the temple, as the agents fired from the table under which Lugs was hiding.

30

SOUNDING their tin whistles, the police van and the ambulance came racing to the Bouillon.

Officers Monti and Deschamps lined the survivors against the wall: Eddie Collins, Jerry Synnott, and Lugs, who was pulled from under the table where he had fallen when the shooting began. 'Genie Etoile got a wall of her own.

The ambulance men came and threw blankets over the remains of Pierre and the Scarperer and took them away on stretchers.

'You four,' said Monti to the prisoners, 'to the salad waggon.' They were escorted to the Black Maria, and Deschamps walked to the police station with Hugh and Aunt Jeannie and Nancy.

They were congratulated and thanked for their services in helping to capture Pierre le Fou, though Aunt Jeannie puzzled them not a little with her references to horses. They knew Ireland's attachment to man's best friend, but assured her that Pierre had little to do with horses, unless it would be a few thousand francs on the Pari Mutuel.

'But they were the wrong men. I was shouting at them and blaming them for something of which they were innocent.'

Lugs stood abject and mourning in the cage.

'I should really apologise to that poor man.'

She stood before Lugs' cage. 'I'm sorry, I...'

'Go away or I'll bite you,' said Lugs, sulkily.

148

The police also explained to Hugh that there was a reward of five million francs in the case of Pierre.

'Oh, I don't want it,' said Aunt Jeannie. 'Let that old man have it.'

'Yes,' said Hugh, 'the Bonapartist.'

'But where is he?' asked Nancy.

' 'Soir, m'sieu, m'dames,' said a soft voice behind them.

He stood in the doorway, and Hugh told him of his new riches.

He was too astonished to believe it at first, but after Hugh had explained to the police officers that the Bonapartist was responsible for the arrests and that Aunt Jeannie wished her share of the reward to go to him, he accepted his good fortune with calm dignity.

'What will you buy with your five million?' asked Deschamps, 'a new dome for the Invalides?'

'First,' said the Bonapartist, 'I shall buy a new suit of clothes and a train ticket for a place in the Midi, very far from Paris.'

'It better be,' muttered 'Genie Etoile, from her cage.

'Tut, tut,' said Gardien de la Paix Androclès Monti, reprovingly, 'pray conduct yourself as befits a bereaved gangstress. Otherwise, I might turn the hose on you.'

When they came out into the air, Nancy remembered that none of them had had dinner.

'As for me,' said Aunt Jeannie, 'it's not what I call it. My evening meal is supper. But no matter what we call it, I haven't eaten anything since lunch.'

Hugh suggested that they go somewhere and have a meal. The Brasserie Lipp, say. They didn't say. Nancy wanted them all to go back to her place.

'The pension, child?' said Aunt Jeannie. 'For a lady that's just refused five thousand pounds?'

'The Lipp, then?' said Hugh.

'Yes,' said Aunt Jeannie. 'You and I can come to some amicable arrangement about money, but tonight I feel I

must let myself go. After that affair in the café, none of us can ever be the same again.'

'That's certainly true of the two fellows they carried off to the morgue,' said Hugh.

'Yes,' said Aunt Jeannie, with a sigh, 'maybe that's what's troubling me.'

'Oh, I didn't mean that,' said Hugh. 'They were two killers themselves. It was better for——'

'One of them to be killed by the official killers?'

'Well, it just happened.'

'It just happened that instead of preventing men's cruelty to dumb beasts, I was assisting at the mystery of their cruelty to each other.'

'Well, we all were put in the way of helping the police.'

'Let us go and eat and drink and we'll——'

'Forget it.'

'Jerry.'

'Don't talk too much, Lugs. That geezer is listening to us. The one at the desk.'

'He doesn't speak English.'

'How do you know?'

'Hey, you frog rat jackamanstink from the back of the pipes,' he looked at the policeman.

'Comment?' said the policeman.

'It's all right, sir,' said Lugs, with a gesture of resignation. 'There, Jerry, what did I tell you?'

'What were you going to say?'

'Do they still have the guillotine over here?'

'Is that all that's worrying you? You needn't bother about the French. They've got nothing on us.'

'I understand a bit of their chat,' said Eddie Collins from his cage, 'and your man told the other fellow there's law coming over from Dublin tomorrow to collect us.'

'Well, thank Crippen for that,' said Lugs. 'If you two

geezers are topped, it'll be the 'Joy, and Pierrepoint will be nice and homely.'

'You're a frit pig,' laughed Eddie Collins. 'They'll have to carry you out if you're topped.'

'Everyone's frit of things like that,' said Lugs. 'But I am frit by nature. I am the cowardliest man ever put foot in this cage and anything I ever done was only for the money.'

In a religious hostel off the rue du Bac were some travellers just arrived from Lourdes and on their way home to Ireland.

'It was on the wireless, Richie, that an Irishman was after being shot in Paris.'

He looked at the old woman.

'You weren't long learning to listen to the wireless in French.'

'The nun told me. She's a Kilkenny woman, being over here for forty years. Not far from here, she said, only up the street. A row between robbers and policemen. This poor Irish fellow was killed stone dead.'

'I hope it wasn't your friend of the plane, that we met on the way over, that gave you the brandy.'

'God forgive you, what a thing to say. A lovely gentleman like that to be mixed up with either robbers or police. It reminds me to say a prayer for him.'

'Say it then. I'm going to put out the light. We've a long road before us tomorrow.'

In Mountjoy a boy turned over, half waking, and thought of the six months he had to do. If only he'd got out with those fellows last month. But what would fellows like that want with a kid the likes of him?

At three in the afternoon, Lugs, Eddie Collins, and Jerry Synnott were brought to an office, where they were met by four Irish detectives, who gave them cigarettes and told them they were being brought back to Dublin on a murder charge.

'Not me,' said Lugs, fearfully. 'I was down below. I was too sick to go up when they threw him overboard. I—I—I——'

'We'll see about the fellow was thrown overboard later,' said the detective in charge, 'but we can only hang you once. Just now we want you on a charge of murdering one James Guiney, by administering to him, or causing to be administered to him, a noxious substance, to wit chloroform——'

'Tralee Trembles,' said Jerry Synnott.

'He trembles no more,' said the detective. 'Not like poor old Lugs here.'

'Leave me alone,' said Lugs, reproachfully, 'and be a bit civilised.'

'And before we step off for our native aeroplane, there's a charge of counterfeiting against you all. Possession including what the dead fellow had in the suitcase and what yous had in your pockets, of fifty-three million thousand francs, forged. That's a matter for the French phoney-note squad. After we're done with you.'

'Forged!'

'Forged!' said Jerry. 'Forged! Well the . . . the dirty crook!'